THE TRAVELER'S
GUIDE TO CLASSICAL
PHILOSOPHY

JOHN GASKIN

THE TRAVELER'S GUIDE TO CLASSICAL PHILOSOPHY

WITH 21 ILLUSTRATIONS

Thames & Hudson

First published in 2011 in paperback in the United States of America by
Thames & Hudson Inc., 500 Fifth Avenue, New York, New York 10110

thamesandhudsonusa.com

Library of Congress Catalog Card Number 2010936808

ISBN 978-0-500-28934-1

Printed and bound in China by Toppan Leefung

938
G212

CONTENTS

Note to the Reader

This book began as a few extemporary lectures, but, encouraged by the remarkable company of men and women who heard me talk about Classical philosophy in some of the great Hellenic theatres of Asia Minor in 2002, and others every year since, I have now tried to present in print what is more easily brought to life through the excitement of the spoken word.

The result is more detailed than the original lectures could have been, and perhaps a little more cautious in its conclusions. But the general structure is the same, and so are the intentions: that the founding ideas of our civilization should be better known; that they should inspire the interest they deserve; and that their relevance to us now should be seen anew.

Use and content
The three parts of this book may be referred to in any order, and internal continuity is intended only in Part II.

Part I contains brief articles on five subjects that may raise questions for travellers in antique lands. The first two chapters try to present a picture in which later details, and much of what you will see on the ground, can find a place.

Part II, on the philosophers, follows a historical sequence. The first two chapters, on Troy and Homer, are in a narrow sense not on philosophers at all, you will say. But in them is the background to all that is thought and felt later. Chapter 10 tries to give some hint of an answer to the question 'How did it all end?'

Part III is a gazetteer of ancient places, with particular reference to the men (and sadly only one woman) who came from them.

Greek and Latin
The Greek ending -*on* (as in Pergamon) became -*um* (Pergamum) in Latin, and the Greek -*os* (as in Ephesos) became the Latin -*us* (Ephesus). The two forms appear interchangeably in this book, according to whichever usage appears to be current in modern English. When there are distinctly different Latin and Greek names for the

same place (with corresponding differences in the anglicized versions, as with Troy/Ilium), either both forms are given, or simply the one most easily recognized.

Sources and acknowledgments

There are numerous brief quotations from ancient authors embedded in the text, the sources of which will be understood from the context. Of those that stand alone, the majority are drawn from the admirable volumes of the Loeb Classical Library, published by Harvard University Press, which describe themselves as 'the only existing series of books which, through original text and English translation, gives access to all that is important in Greek and Latin literature'. Quotations are sometimes abbreviated or given in a new translation.

Quotations from Homer's *Iliad* are from the Oxford World's Classics translation by Robert Fitzgerald (1998). Their location is given by reference to the traditional book numbers and lines of verse.

Quotations from Plato are in the revered translation by Benjamin Jowett, originally published in 1871 (Oxford, 4th edn 1953).

Verse translations from Lucretius are drawn from the almost unobtainable paraphrase of parts of the original by W. H. Mallock (*Lucretius on Life and Death*; London, 1900). All the quotations from Epicurus can be found in my *The Epicurean Philosophers* (London, 1995), while those from Diogenes of Oinoanda are from Martin Ferguson Smith's book *The Epicurean Inscription* (Naples, 1993).

In general, ancient writings of any length were divided into 'books' – the amount that could be contained within a single papyrus roll – which were about the length of a long chapter in a modern book. Wherever practical I have cited the number of the book in which a quotation appears, and also the section within the book (if it has sections).

PART I

The Idea of Hellenism: What the Greeks Created

1

The Scheme
of Things Entire

Historical speculation is fun; dates and facts are often thought of as tedious. But in their absence there is no structure, no framework in which to fit one's experience of things past. In the case of Classical antiquity, the very simplistic outline set out below may help. It begins with the independent Hellenic cities of the Aegean and the Greek mainland in the 8th century BC, and charts the spread of Hellenism through their founding of colonies. It continues with Alexander's conquests and the dominions of his successors, which are followed by the generally benign attitude of the Romans towards Hellenic culture. We then move through the slow disintegration of the Roman Empire, to conclude with the transformation of Classicism into Byzantine Christianity in the 4th century AD.

The Archaic Age: Ionian cities and colonies, c. 750–547 BC

This is the era when numerous small, free, independent Hellenic cities – most conspicuously Miletus – prospered, founding colonies (settlements related to the mother city) on the coasts of the Black Sea, the Sea of Marmara, Asia Minor, North Africa and southern Italy. Latterly the chief mainland power in western Asia Minor was Lydia.

c. 750–675	Homer creates the *Iliad* and the *Odyssey*. Hesiod writes.
c. 625–547	Miletus flourishes. Thales and others begin the first enquiry into the physical nature of the universe.
560–547	Croesus is king of Lydia.
547	Cyrus the Great, king of the Persians, takes Lydia and numerous Ionian cities.

The Classical Age: Persian Wars, Athens and Sparta, 547–334 BC

This period is usually regarded as the core of Classical antiquity. It is dominated by wars between Persia and various alliances of Greek cities, by the cultural achievements of Athens, and by the Peloponnesian Wars between Athens and Sparta. In its last seventy years, it saw something like a cold war between Persia and various Greeks, and in Caria (south-western Asia Minor) the emergence of the Hecatomnid dynasty, nominally subject to Persia but a Hellenizing influence. The Mausoleum at Halicarnassus is its best-known product. The history of the Persian Wars is provided by Herodotus.

499	Ionian revolt against Persia.
494	Hellenic fleet loses the sea battle of Lade; sack of Miletus.
490	First Persian expedition to mainland Greece, under Darius. Persians defeated in the battle of Marathon.
480	Second Persian expedition to mainland Greece, under Xerxes. Spartans lose the fiercely contested battle of Thermopylae. Most of the Persian fleet is destroyed in the sea battle of Salamis. Athens is evacuated, and the 'old' acropolis is destroyed by the Persians. Xerxes retires to Asia leaving his army to overwinter in Thessaly.
479	Greek counter-attack and victory in the land battle of Plataea and in the decisive sea battle off Cape Mycale.
478–431	Rise of the Athenian Empire, and the age of Pericles. Parthenon built. Great dramatists at work in Athens. Athenian democracy at its height.
c. 467	Land and sea battle at the river Eurymedon ends active Persian threat to Greeks; thereafter, Persian kings rely on gold and diplomacy to maintain their western empire.
432–404	Peloponnesian Wars between Sparta and Athens, as recorded by Thucydides. Final defeat of Athens in 404.
404–347	Plato working in Athens.
404–334	Armed hostility between mainland Greece (Sparta) and Persia in protracted 'cold war'.
399	Death of Socrates.
377–334	Hecatomnid dynasty in Caria Hellenizes area under nominal Persian suzerainty.

Alexander the Great of Macedonia and the destruction of the Persian Empire, 334–323 BC

340–323	Aristotle working in Athens.
334	Battle of Granicus gives Alexander opportunity to take most of Asia Minor.
333	Battle of Issus allows Alexander to take Egypt.
331	Battle of Gaugamela ends in the flight of Darius III. Alexander sets out to conquer the world to the east.
323	Death of Alexander the Great in Babylon.
322	Aristotle dies in Chalcis.

The Hellenistic Age and the rise of Rome, 323–31 BC

After the death of Alexander, his vast conquests were divided, not always peacefully, between his generals and his companions. This resulted in the spread of Hellenistic culture over wide areas of the eastern Mediterranean and as far east as the borders of India. Conspicuous among his successors were the Ptolemies, who ruled an extended Egypt, and the Seleucids, who reigned over Asia Minor and lands initially extending to modern Afghanistan. Almost by accident, the west of Asia Minor became a kingdom under the control of the rich and eccentric Attalids of Pergamon, the last of whom, Attalus III, bequeathed his kingdom to Rome with remarkable foresight of the shape of things to come.

331–on	Athens becomes the philosophical capital of Western world with the establishment of schools founded by Plato, Aristotle, and the Epicureans and the Stoics.
146	Macedonia and mainland Greece become Roman provinces.
130	Roman province of Asia (Asia Minor) created.
88–85	Mithridates VI, king of Pontus, overruns Roman Asia Minor. Greek cities variously side with him or with Rome, to their cost or advantage.
44	Murder of Julius Caesar.
44–31	Roman civil wars, involving Mark Antony against Brutus and Cassius (Mark Antony is victorious at the battle of Philippi, 42 BC), and then Mark Antony against Octavius.

| 31 | Battle of Actium. Octavius becomes master of the Roman world. |
| 30 | Cleopatra, last Ptolemy of Egypt and ally of Antony, kills herself. |

Pax Romana: The empire of Rome, 30 BC to 2nd century AD

In 30 BC Octavius began the process that established Rome as a power governed by an emperor. In the first eighty years after the death of Augustus (Octavius) in AD 14, this produced a series of rulers that varied between the abominable, the competent and the highly success-ful, while in territory the empire expanded and remained unchallenged in any serious way.

In the 2nd century AD – the 'century of peace', as it has sometimes been called – a succession of men of ability and dedication ruled at the apex of Roman power. Their names and dates as emperor are:

96–98	Nerva
98–118	Trajan
118–138	Hadrian
138–161	Antoninus
161–180	Marcus Aurelius

Hadrian in particular is a name you will meet again and again, from the North Tyne in north-east England to Aswan in southern Egypt. He travelled everywhere, embellished cities, beautified the world and defended his vast dominions; but within twenty years of his death, the threat from the north re-emerged, and Marcus Aurelius, the great Stoic, was concerned more with defending the empire, internally still at peace, than with enjoying it by travel.

Danger and division, AD 200–395

In the 3rd century AD the break up of the empire seemed always at hand but never happened. There was a succession of weak emperors put in place by the army and too briefly in charge to be effective; Goths invaded from the north (repelled with difficulty), and there was an ever increasing threat from German tribes. Christians were subject to erratic and occasional persecution, which resulted in a challenge to the focus of allegiance in the empire. Economic dislocation became widespread.

Diocletian, who ruled from 285 until he retired in 305, made heroic efforts to reform the economic and political structure of the empire and to reaffirm its ancient religious structures. Some of his reforms were carried through by Constantine the Great (r. 306–337), who asserted Christianity as the official religion of the empire while clearly permitting the continuation of other religions and forms of worship.

337   Byzantium is refounded as Constantinople. Intended to be the New Rome, it rapidly becomes a New Jerusalem.

337–395 Evolution of a split between the Western Empire in Rome and an Eastern Empire in Constantinople.

361–363 Emperor Julianus (Julian) makes a final attempt as a pagan to accommodate Christianity and other religions.

379–395 Reign of Theodosius I. Final separation of Eastern and Western Empires, and the enforcement of Christianity as the only religion of the Eastern (Byzantine) Empire.

An entry in *Chambers Dictionary of Biography* speaks of Theodosius thus: 'A pious and intolerant Christian, he summoned in 381 a council at Constantinople to affirm the Nicene Creed, pursued heretics and pagans, and eventually in 391 ordered the closure of all temples and banned all non-Christian forms of religion.' He also closed all theatres and *gymnasia* (schools), and prohibited the Olympic games. It only remained for the Emperor Justinian, in 529, to order the closure of the remaining non-Christian schools of philosophy in Athens – those devoted to Neoplatonism – and the Classical world was at an end.

2

The Idea of Hellenism

> 'Are you coming with us tomorrow to see Alinda?' enquired the Learned Doctor.
>
> 'Some such name,' said the Personality brightly. 'Although I thought it was Alabanda. There's probably not much difference. When you've seen one ruin you've seen them all.'
>
> – John Gaskin, 'From Lydia with Love and Laughter' (2006)

The Learned Doctor's outraged intake of breath at such crass cynicism was justified, but anyone who has seen the ruins of more than two or three Hellenic cities (of course not including such very ancient sites as Troy and Mycenae) will have some sympathy with the Personality. In some ways, and for a good reason, the cities from Elea to Alexandria *are* all similar.

The sites resemble each other because they all have a set of structures in common. These structures result from the political and cultural activities that constituted being Greek: the idea of Hellenism. The earliest literary record of such an idea occurs in Book VIII of Herodotus' *The Persian Wars*, written *c.* 430–420 BC, where an Athenian speaks of 'the kinship of all Hellenes in blood and speech, and the shrines of gods and the sacrifices we have in common, and the likeness of our way of life'. About half a century later Isocrates, the Athenian orator and political theorist, opens out the concept of Hellenism beyond that of blood ties: 'The name Hellene no longer suggests a race, but an intelligence, and the title "Hellenes" is applied rather to those who share our culture, than to those who share a common blood' (from his discourse *Panegyricus*).

What was it to 'share a culture'? It was to be a member of a *polis* – a settlement wholly or at least partly free from outside domination, organized according to a written constitution that contained some democratic elements. The pattern typically involved a city with a *prytaneion*, a dining hall or town hall for entertaining guests or emissaries from other cities; a *boule* or ruling council, which met in a designated building, the *bouleuterion*; and an *ekklesia*, or public assembly, which met in the theatre. The *boule* conducted the day-to-day business of the city and appointed magistrates responsible for defence, aquaducts, markets, festivals, public games, civic buildings, outlying territory, and so on.

To be a Hellenic city was to have a theatre big enough to seat most of the citizens for the purpose of public meetings, trials, plays, festivals and other large-scale theatrical entertainments. It was to participate in inter-city games and musical competitions, and in the great pan-Hellenic Olympic Games. It was to have a common, but not exclusive, group of gods – the Olympians – one of whom would usually be the patron or protector of the city, and it was to have Greek at least as the lingua franca. It was to have schools (*gymnasia*) where boys were taught to read and write and speak in public, and where they developed their military and athletic skills; this explains the presence of the stadium, which was often outside the city walls or near to the gymnasium itself. Finally, it was to have a certain social system: citizens, free foreign visitors and residents, and slaves (or kept servants). There was a close-knit family life, and for the men a social life that centred upon the convention-regulated banquet or *symposium*.

What I have outlined above originated in the 5th century BC or earlier, but persisted with changes well into the 2nd century AD. The

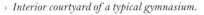
Interior courtyard of a typical gymnasium.

notion of citizenship in particular expands in proportion to the larger political structure of the world: in the 2nd century AD, you will find memorials proudly recording the dead person as a citizen of Rome, of Caria (for example), and of a particular city. In the eastern half of the Roman Empire, Greek extended its hold as the language of commerce and as the lingua franca, but the idea of Hellenism became more that of a cultured elite, more literary, as the world became more precarious, despotic, large-scale, religiously dogmatic and hostile to constitutional democracy. Synesius of Cyrene (c. AD 370–413) – possibly a Christian, but certainly a man who deplored the decline of humane culture – defended a pagan or Hellenic Greek as 'one able to associate with men on the basis of a knowledge of all worthwhile literature' – a shrivelled but still not ignoble concept that survived into the 1960s.

So being a Hellenic *polis* necessarily involved having a certain set of buildings in common:

an *agora* – the forum or marketplace. The *agora* would be built as splendidly as the city could afford: a large paved square or oblong, sometimes with a shrine in the middle, surrounded by a colonnade behind which are shops and stalls with their stock rooms to the rear or below.

city walls – a defensive system that surrounded the city. Often pre-dating 30 BC, the walls were constructed from large, finely-fitting blocks of stone without cement joins ('ashlar masonry'). These were largely redundant at the height of Pax Romana, but were often restored and augmented in the 3rd century AD. They are always massive, and make the walls of medieval Europe look like rubble-and-mortar constructions.

an aqueduct – a manmade water supply that ran overhead on arches, was piped below ground or followed the contours of a hill. The aqueduct usually arrived at an elaborate distribution point within the city, which was sometimes ornately decorated and spectacularly presented by the Romans as a *nymphaeum*, with statues, fountains and pools. See examples at Miletus, Lepcis Magna, Carthage, and the upper city of Ephesus (to the left as you enter from the top).

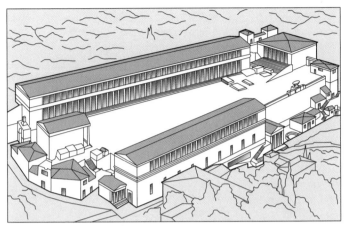

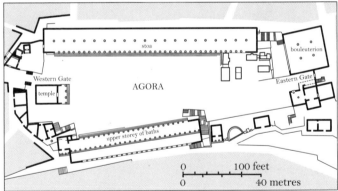

The city of Assos, showing public buildings of the Classical period.

a bath house – a large complex of arches, rooms, pools and heating systems. Bath houses were always Roman additions to the original Hellenic city. The Hellenes did wash, and had domestic water systems for fresh water and sewage, but they did not have the vast hedonistic extravaganzas introduced by the Romans almost as a way of life.

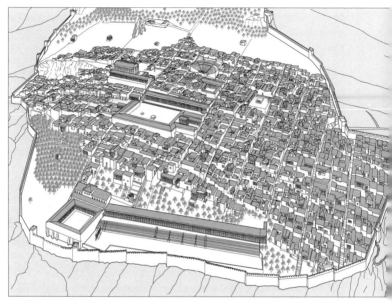

Priene as a Hellenistic city, with its regular arrangement of streets.

cisterns – underground chambers for the storage of water. Traces of the pink waterproof cement with which they were lined are often still visible. But walk warily (in Alinda, perhaps): if you fall into one and live long enough to know that you have done so, you may have a considerable wait before anyone notices you deep below the ground. In the wilderness of Lydai there is one, said to be Byzantine, into which I almost fear to look.

a Hippodamian grid plan – a regular plan of squares according to which city streets were laid out. This arrangement is conspicuous at Priene, but also evident in some other sites.

a stadium – an enclosed running track, typically with rounded ends and tiers of seating. It was used for athletic sports and races, and also sometimes for chariot racing – particularly under later Roman influence.

a *bouleuterion* – the meeting place of the city council. It was small enough to be roofed over, but in its ruinous state is difficult to distinguish from an *odeon*. The odeon took the form of an intimate theatre (a fine example is at Aphrodisias) for musical recitals, declamations of poetry, small meetings, and so on, where the audience would be in the region of one hundred people. (Theatres could seat up to twenty thousand or more.) The *bouleuterion* is sometimes a half-circle, like the *odeon* (e.g. at Nysa), but sometimes it takes the form of an oblong or right-angled horseshoe, with the fourth side open for access from the corners and with the speaker's position in the middle (e.g. at Priene).

Sometimes there is also an *asclepium* – an area that could include a temple, a hospital and other buildings sacred to Asclepius, the god of healing and medicine. Celebrated examples are at Kos and Pergamon. The treatment comprised a combination of cleansing, resting, sleep, prayer and gentle medicine, and often resulted in the sort of cures still variously described as faith healing or miracles.

There is one last feature of the Hellenic, and later the Roman, city that cannot be seen as such, but that greatly enhanced what can be seen. These cities were rivals – not merely in trade and games and sometimes in fighting, but in appearance. To have bigger, better-presented

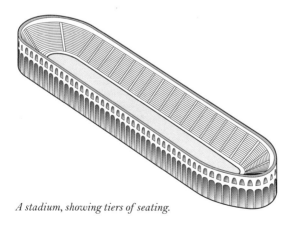

A stadium, showing tiers of seating.

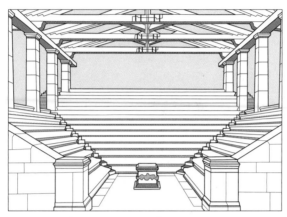

Reconstructed interior of a council house, or bouleuterion.

or more finely embellished buildings than your rival was to score a point, to be a more notable place. The activity of Hellenistic kings set the precedent. Their civic improvements were emulated by Roman emperors – notably Hadrian – and followed by the successful citizen who had benefited from the city that reared him or her and sought to return something to it. It was a double process in which the city gained endowments and the donor won public approval. A similar process operated in Victorian Britain, and still holds good in the United States.

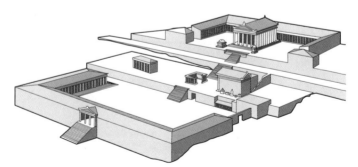

Reconstruction of the Asclepium at Kos.

3

Wine, Sex and the Symposium

Greek family customs differed from city to city, but Athens was typical. There was a close family, whose relationships were enshrined in law and custom, and there was an extended family held together by lesser obligations. Marriage was arranged between the parents of the bride and the parents of the groom. The bride was usually about 15 years old, and the groom about 30. Marriage was for life, and divorce was uncommon, although quite easy for a man and not impossibly difficult for a woman. The man dealt with public business, wars, and providing for his family. The woman had almost complete control over all domestic affairs. Domestic servants would be owned slaves – a system that continued wherever there were conquerors and conquered for another two and a half thousand years, regardless of new religions and social changes.

Since inheritance, citizenship and headship of a family depended upon certainty about the parentage of children, extra-marital sex for married women was forbidden; although not forbidden for men, it could be regarded as a good reason for the wife to petition for a divorce. So in general the family unit was secure and protected. We hear almost nothing about incest in Classical culture.

Eros

Modern conceptions of homosexuality, heterosexuality and paedophilia do not fit the Classical world. There was simply no moral issue with homosexuality, although there were well-observed conventions; paedophilia involving young children was probably very rare indeed, partly because of the matriarchal control of family life, partly because of other sexual freedoms and conventions we do not have. Well-reared boys or young men roughly between the ages of 14 and 18 were expected to have men between the ages of about 18 and about 30 (that is, marrying age) as social and intellectual mentors, lovers, hero-figures, and physically close friends who, with agreement, practised *eros*. At about the age of eighteen the roles were reversed, and the loved became lovers. What we, in about the last five minutes of Western cultural history, have come to call 'same-sex marriages' – permanent adult relationships – were rare, regarded as effeminate or somewhat ridiculous and otherwise ignored.

Prostitution (male and female) was common and not illegal, but neither was it regarded as a suitable occupation for a free-born citizen. So it was that the majority of prostitutes were slaves or freed slaves. A recent writer has calculated that they charged 'about the same as today' – whatever that may add up to. Syphilis and AIDS did not exist in the Classical world.

One last thought about Hellenic sexual attitudes (which may have already occurred to you): people in the Classical world were enormously less inhibited than we are, even after the 'sexual revolution' of the past fifty years. Dionysus was fêted in public as the god of wine and sex – the earliest origin of theatrical religious rites. His son, Priapus, often represented as a grotesquely humanized version of an erect phallus, caused so little embarrassment, let alone condemnation, that he often featured as a garden ornament or as an object of amusement. Nakedness, particularly male nakedness – for example during athletics, games or while bathing – was entirely normal: erotic and provoking possibly, but entirely normal and common all the same. So there was no need for pornography, except as a joke, and there was no need for sexually explicit literature when sexuality was normal and obvious.

The process of change began in earnest with Theodosius at the end of the 4th century AD, but it took many more years of religious teaching to make nakedness embarrassing, celibacy and abstinence a virtue, same-sex love a sin, and for little or nothing to be sayable – at least easily – about sex. As a result, Freud may have been right in his views on sexual repression at the end of the 19th century. He would certainly have been laughed to scorn in the Athens of Pericles or in the Rome of Hadrian. Repression? What's that? But try as we may, we cannot now retrieve the freedoms of the Classical world. At best we can look back with surprise, and perhaps with regret for the loss of its naturalism and simplicity. At least we can refrain from condemning what we have been taught not to understand.

The symposium

The symposium played a central role in the social life of men in Archaic and Classical Greece, and for many centuries after. It was a highly mannered wine-dominated gathering of men who had military, social or political bonds, and it was held for the purpose of drinking, discussion, and musical and erotic entertainment. But it would usually be preceded by the family *deipnon*, or dinner. A description so vivid that one can almost picture the scene is preserved by Athenaeus in a fragment of poetry by Xenophanes. It dates from about 540 BC.

> For now the floor is clean, as are everyone's hands and the cups. One attendant places woven garlands round our heads, while another offers us fragrant perfume in a bowl; and a mixing-bowl full of good cheer stands in the middle. Another kind of wine, sweet as honey and smelling of flowers, is ready in the jars, and promises we will never exhaust it. In our midst is frankincense that produces a sacred scent; and the water is cold, delicious and pure. Golden-brown loaves of bread have been set beside us along with a table laden with cheese and dense honey. In the middle is an altar covered on all sides with flowers: song and dance and celebration fill the house. It is proper for reasonable men to begin by offering a hymn to the god's honour, using decent stories and pure words. But when they have poured a libation and prayed for the power to do what is just, it is no disgrace to drink as much as will enable you to return home without a guide – unless you are very old!

The Classical symposium – much depicted on pottery and described by ancient authors from Xenophon in the 5th century BC to Athenaeus at the end of the 2nd century AD – became much more elaborate than this Archaic meal. It was held in a men's room – an *andron* – specifically designed for the purpose, with couches set round its sides where men reclined singly or in pairs, and with tables set in front of them. The entrance door was always off-centre, to allow for an uneven number of couches: rooms with seven, nine and fifteen couches have been found.

It is not known when or why the Homeric manner of eating and drinking – at tables and chairs – changed into the (apparently less comfortable) fashion of reclining, but there is some evidence that it developed in imitation of Near Eastern habits. Amid the general denunciations of the prophet Amos, in about 750 BC, is this:

> Woe to those who lie upon beds of ivory, and stretch
> themselves upon their couches, and eat lambs from the flock,
> and calves from the midst of the stall; who sing idle songs to
> the sound of the harp, and like David invent for themselves
> instruments of music; who drink wine in bowls ... the revelry
> of those that stretch themselves shall pass away. (Amos 6: 6–8)

If you subtract the lamb and calves, this could be an outline description of the later Greek symposium, which did not pass away until a thousand years after the demise of Amos. But the gathering became much more formalized.

The fraternity of the guests was reinforced through drinking and the enjoyment of ritualized friendship: a flute girl would play; wine in open communal cups would be passed around by naked boys; the participants would sing with head and an arm held up; and the late arrival could enter only with permission, and possibly with a forfeit. There would often be a director of wine to ensure that each guest drank a just amount – not too much and not too little; and there would be contests, such as the game in which participants threw a single drop of wine from their bowl into a central dish, the successful thrower winning his lover. The wine was always mixed with water, and drunk in large quantities like beer.

Wine

We know more about Greek wine and the customs surrounding its consumption than we do about any other social habit in antiquity. This is on account of the surviving writings of just one man – Athenaeus – who flourished about AD 190. He must have had either an immense library or an absolutely phenomenal memory, for his long book *The Learned Banqueters*, or the *Deipnosophists*, contains thousands of quotations from ancient authors that are produced for the instruction and entertainment of the symposiasts. Books X and XI are almost entirely concerned with wine and drinking. We learn that there was much debate about the correct proportion of wine to water (about one to three seems to be average), whether it should be passed from right to left or from left to right, whether a large open bowl should be circulated or smaller individual cups used, and about their correct shape. Above all, the emphasis again and again is on drinking generously but not to excess. Athenaeus is a wonderful mine of anecdotes but, as with all mines, some of what is dug up is dross. A few nuggets will give an idea of what is there.

On drinking wine unmixed with water:

> If only we had the hangover before we got drunk, no one
> would ever consume more wine than he should. But as it is
> we forget there's a penalty for getting drunk – so we drink
> unmixed wine!

And again, concerning 'Scythian drinking' (from southern Russia), quoting Anacreon:

> Come on – let's not indulge in Scythian drinking any
> longer with banging and shouting; let's drink a little
> to the accompaniment of beautiful hymns.

And on Athenian moderation:

> You see, this is the Hellenic way of drinking – use cups
> of modest size, have some banter and pleasant conversation
> with one another. The other way amounts to bathing,
> not drinking. I mean drinking from a wine-cooling vessel
> or buckets – not drinking, but death-dealing.

And again:

> A mark of a free man is to drink one's wine carefully, not
> consuming large amounts at one time, or gulping without
> time to breath as the Thracians do, but mixing conversation
> into drinking as medicines into life to keep you healthy.

Good advice:

> The fact is that some people suffer considerable physical and
> mental damage when they drink large quantities of unmixed
> wine at parties … Keep three things in mind when you drink
> large amounts. Do not drink low-quality wine. Do not drink
> undiluted wine. Do not eat snacks of food with the wine.

And lastly, because it says so much in a light-hearted way about the
Greek sense of the brevity of life, so evident at the beginning in Homer,
and so enduring in Classical antiquity:

> We're not hurting people around us, so don't you realize that
> this 'life', as it's called, is just a word designed to amuse us, a
> nice way of referring to our fate as human beings? This is my
> conclusion: human existence is entirely idiotic, and as long as
> we're alive, we're enjoying a reprieve, like going to a festival;
> we've been released from death and darkness, and allowed
> to have a party in the light. And whoever laughs the most,
> and drinks the most, and seizes Aphrodite while he is free …
> he's the happiest when he gets home after the festival.

Athenaeus is quoting Alexis, a writer of numerous comic plays who
lived *c.* 350–275 BC. None of his works survive. Books X and XI of
Athenaeus can be found in vol. V of the Loeb edition of his works
(Cambridge, Mass., 2009).

4

Theatres: Festivals, Entertainments and Meetings

As I was standing in the extensive ruins of a large theatre in a rather small city, someone said to me, 'How on earth could they justify the economic outlay on something like this for the occasional performance of a play?' The short answer is that theatres were used not just for occasional theatrical entertainments. In the nine hundred years from their first development in the 5th century BC until their forced closure in the eastern Roman Empire by Theodosius in about AD 395, theatres had many functions, and showed many architectural variations on the basic shape.

The structures

The earliest 'theatres' (which you will not see) were probably no more than carts drawn up on one side of an open space – like the agora, for example. The first recognizable type of theatre, which used a hillside for the seating and a flat area at its foot for the action, developed at the end of the 6th century BC. This flat area was rapidly formalized into a circular space – the *orchestra*, or dancing floor (the Greek word *orchestra* means 'dance') – while the hillside was crafted into the familiar horse-shoe dish to hold seating; the Greeks referred to the auditorium as the *theatron*, while the Romans knew it as the *cavea*.

By the end of the 5th century BC the typical Hellenic theatre had fully evolved. The audience sat on the tiers of stone seats in the auditorium, which is divided into segments by flights of steps. The tiers of seats are divided horizontally by walkways, or *diazomata*. The *theatron* in Hellenic theatres (not in Roman) is always a little larger than a semi-circle: the ends of the seating area extend beyond the central point, giving it the general shape of a horseshoe. Each end of the *theatron* terminates in a retaining wall, the *analemma*. The horseshoe encloses a circular *orchestra*, and on the open side, opposite the audience, is the stage, or *proskenion*, which was originally at the same level as the orchestra but was soon raised to become an oblong platform a few feet higher. It is backed by the *skene*, the low buildings that allowed performers access to the stage and provided changing rooms and storage. They were usually no more than about 3 metres (10 feet) high. The audience had access to the seating area via two *paradoi* – uncovered gaps at *orchestra* level between the ends of the *theatron* and the stage. In time there was a tendency for the stage to encroach on the *orchestra*, so that its circle became flattened on one side. The best intact example of a Hellenic theatre is at Epidaurus.

The Roman theatre – very often constructed by adapting, or partially adapting, the original Hellenic structure – has the same general shape as the Hellenic, but with changes that give it a very different feel where the stage buildings survive. The *cavea* is shortened back into a half-circle in contrast to the Hellenic horseshoe. The stage buildings abut the ends of the *cavea*, with the result that the *orchestra* becomes a half-circle. The *skene* is raised to the same height as the top of the auditorium, and is joined on to it. This means that the audience has to get in and out by means of large tunnels and steps, known by the somewhat unfortunate Latin title *vomitaria*. Superb examples are at Miletus.

The Roman *skene* was solid stone, embellished with columns, niches, statues and other decorations; and it was strong enough to support a tent-like roof structure on poles, which protected the audience from the sun and provided the means for theatrical effects, such as making a god fly above the stage (the original *deus ex machina*). In Hellenic theatres, the audience – except those in the lowest rows of seats – could always see out over the stage to the country beyond. In Roman theatres, however, the audience was in effect completely enclosed and could see only the actors and scenery, as in a modern theatre. An almost perfect example of a Roman theatre can be seen at Aspendos, in southern Turkey.

In Roman theatres, and in Roman adaptions of Hellenic originals, you will often see that the lowest two levels of seats have been removed to allow for a wall between the *orchestra* and the *cavea*. This indicates that the theatre was used for entertainments involving dangerous animals, gladiators or simulated water battles.

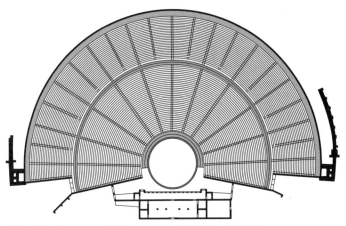

Plan of the theatre at Epidaurus, a typical Hellenistic design.

I have described the two types of theatre as if they are always clearly distinct. They are not. In numerous cases the structures have been only partly modified, and almost every variation between the pure Hellenic and the pure Roman theatre exists somewhere.

How the theatres were used

Drama in Athens evolved from religious festivals, chief of which was the great spring Dionysia. In part, this festival was celebrated through the performance of what came to be called 'tragedies' – semi-dramatic stories from Homer and other epic sources. The tragedies were joined in about 488 BC by comedies – a type of performance that had already existed for some time elsewhere in the Greek world. As soon as there were such plays, there followed the familiar theatrical trappings – masks, music, commentaries by the chorus, actors, applause and rivalry (the poets competed for prizes).

The early tragedies have an extreme ritualistic formality in performance, and a slow, almost fatalistic progression, like a dead march. The actors' dialogue is stylized, they are few in number, and there is always a chorus commentating on or explaining the action. The names of Aeschylus, Sophocles and Euripides (the youngest of the three), all of whom worked in the 5th century BC, will be forever known, despite the fact that so many of their works are lost. The last extant play of Euripides, the *Bacchae*, must stand among the greatest and most disturbing stage works ever written.

The first tragedies were all on epic or legendary themes, while the comedies of Aristophanes were all based on contemporary political issues. It was apparently Agathon (who features in Plato's *Symposium*), at the very end of the 5th century BC, who first wrote tragedies with invented plots and characters, but nothing of his work survives beyond a few quotations.

By the 3rd century BC plays were less religious, less political, less profound, more domestic and more for entertainment. The works of Menander set the standard for domestic comedy right up until William Congreve, Oscar Wilde and Noel Coward. Menander's plays, which were often performed in Latinized versions by Plautus, and others by known writers whose works are mostly lost continued to be performed throughout antiquity.

Once the plays (particularly the comedies) were detached by use and custom from their original context in religious festivals, what we might call travelling repertory companies came into existence to take them from city to city. The best-known and longest-lasting of such troupes were the Artists of Dionysus – a guild of itinerant Greek actors and musicians formed in the 3rd century BC. In about 200 BC Teos, on the coast of Asia Minor north of Ephesus, became their home. As with so many groups of artists after them, their behaviour was regarded as unacceptable in regular communities, and they were moved on. But they endured, probably until the reign of the emperor Diocletian at the end of the 3rd century AD.

So theatres were used much more than one might suppose for plays and festivals that were at the very heart of the community. In the Roman centuries of antiquity they were also used for mimes (pantomimes are the nearest we get to the idea), and for a variety of large-scale public entertainments – notably for wild animal shows, gladiatorial fights and simulated battles. There was also one overwhelmingly important use not yet mentioned. Almost from start to finish, these theatres were used for public meetings of the sort required by Greek ideas of democracy, and for trials. It is almost certain, for example, that Socrates was tried in a theatre. Public viewing aside, the size of the jury meant that the trial could have been accommodated only in large venue like a theatre. Such public democracy, at least on a local scale, continued in many cities under Roman rule, and for almost any urgent matter that concerned the majority of citizens the theatre was the first place of assembly. The best-known record of such an event is Acts 19: 23–40: some of the tradesmen of Ephesus jumped to the conclusion that Paul's teaching would put them out of business, 'so … they rushed together into the theatre'. The tradesmen were of course partly right, but not for another three hundred and forty years, by which time their trade would be at the service of another god, and their theatres and democracies lost for a thousand years.

5

Temples: Gods, Feasts and Safe Deposits

Try not to look at a temple sacred to Classical gods with the eyes of a Christian or Muslim, seeking similarities to churches or mosques. Its function was entirely different. The pagan devotee prayed, made offerings and offered praise *outside* the temple. Inside was the house of the god, inviolable and to be visited only by the priests, who were usually civic officials appointed for that purpose. (Some sacred places – particularly those where oracles could be consulted – did have permanent priests.) On special occasions the image of the god might be brought out from within the temple, in order for it be seen or to watch an offering; otherwise the god remained hidden – a work of human hands occupied by the power of what was imaged.

In Italy, Sicily, the Lebanon, Syria and even in southern France, it is still possible to find temples with their internal structures more or less in place. In Asia Minor and Greece itself, little usually survives other than tumbled columns and the podium – the stepped platform on which the temple stood.

The temple's general external appearance, with its surrounding rows of single or double-depth columns, will be familiar to everyone. It is what happened inside, and outside at the front, that needs explanation.

Before the temple, outside and free-standing, was the altar: the place where the sacrifice was made to the deity. In many cases this is now only visible, if at all, as a relatively small area of paving on the ground. It is the spot where, during the course of public festivals, the animals were ritually killed and some of the offal, bones and blood burnt so that the smoke could ascend to the god. The meat was then cooked and distributed to the participants as part of a feast. In the case of a large festival, these could be many, demanding a correspondingly large number of animals.

At the front of the temple was a massive door or pair of doors, set into the solid interior walls that were largely concealed by the external rows of columns. These doors completely secured the interior space. They led either directly or via an anteroom to the shrine – the place of the god and of his or her statue. Beyond this again, at the back of the temple, was a further room (or rooms), accessed via the shrine or, more commonly, by means of a smaller but very strong rear door. This was the strongroom or (in Latin) the *cella*: the place that performed almost the function of a safe deposit in a modern city. It was safe in two senses: an intruder would have to violate the place of the god to reach it, and it was the most strongly secured and hidden place in the temple. In it were placed the temple treasures, including the gold and valuables presented to it. The civic treasury and private deposits of valuables were also stored here.

A great deal is not known about the exact use of pagan temples. For example, it is uncertain to what extent the sanctuary was accessible, once the main doors were opened, to visits by worshippers in small

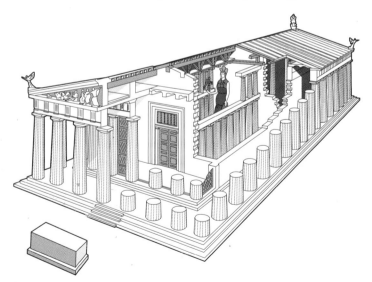

Cut-away reconstruction of a Classical temple.

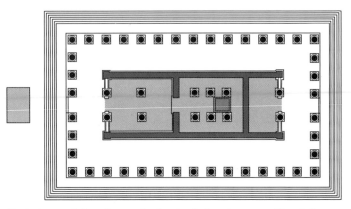

Typical ground plan of a temple, showing its interior spaces: (from left to right) the anteroom, shrine and strongroom.

groups; and it is a moot point whether the image of the god was regarded as a living thing (making its worship real idolatry). There is some evidence that it was, particularly by the ignorant; but there is rather more evidence that the nature and power of the deity were believed to somehow infuse the image. (The same ambiguity exists in the 'worship' of saints and relics in certain Christian traditions.) But it is certain that token offerings were regularly made to the images in the hope of favours or the granting of prayers. It is also certain that temples were used for the making of oaths, a special element in Greek legal commitments, and that a select few – Didyma, Claros, Delphi and Cumae, for example – were regularly consulted as oracles. Remember that there were no holy men. It was the places that were holy.

The gods
Although Classical antiquity was polytheistic, the number of Olympian gods was quite small: Zeus ('father of gods and men'), Hera (his wife), Athena, Apollo, Artemis, Poseidon, Aphrodite, Hermes, Hephaestus and Ares (god of war – the Roman Mars), together with Demeter and Dionysus. In each city one particular god would receive special honours (Athena at Athens, and Artemis at Ephesus, for instance), but not to the

exclusion of others. Coexisting with the Olympians were the gods of the earth and the underworld: Hades, Persephone, the nymphs (and numerous other minor deities of lakes, rivers, forests and mountains), Pan, and the household gods (gods of the hearth).

As the Hellenic world changed into the even larger multicultural and cosmopolitan Roman world, so the tendency to receive new deities into the pantheon of possible gods gathered pace. This trend came particularly from Egypt and the East, but also from the Roman habit of identifying the gods of conquered or protected territories with their own gods, who in turn were mostly the Hellenic gods called by different names. But the gods never excluded each other. In the 2nd century AD one visitor to Didyma, Apollo's great sanctuary, observed how it was encircled by altars to every deity.

Was this plethora of invisible divine beings really believed in? With the sort of qualifications and details so admirably set out in Robin Lane Fox's fine book *Pagans and Christians* (London, 1986), the best brief answer is still the one given by Edward Gibbon:

> The various modes of worship, which prevailed in the
> Roman world, were all considered by the people as equally
> true; by the philosophers as equally false; and by the
> magistrates as equally useful.

* * *

The subjects I have touched upon in the above chapters can be followed in greater detail, together with many other items, in *The Oxford History of the Classical World* (Oxford, 1986): a book written by expert scholars but in a readable form.

PART II

The Ideal of Homer and the Ideas of the Philosophers

1

Troy: The Legend and the Book

Some time around five thousand years ago, human beings established a settlement on a low hill in north-west Asia Minor. In about 1250 BC – nearly two thousand years later – the Trojan War was fought. Some five hundred years after that, a man known as Homer recorded in detail an episode towards the end of that remote and legendary conflict. In 334 BC, at the shrine of Achilles at Troy, Alexander the Great dedicated himself to the overthrow of the Persian Empire. According to Lucian, in 48 BC Julius Caesar visited the site, which was revered by Romans as the place from whence came Aeneas, the legendary Trojan founder of Rome – a place 'now only a famous name … where the very ruins have been destroyed … but where a legend still clings to every stone'. Caesar promised that a Roman Troy should arise. It did. Four hundred years later, the future emperor Julianus Augustus (Julian) discreetly travelled to the place to discover if the ancient rites were still being observed, in a world of new and alien beliefs. They were. Another fifteen hundred years passed, and in 1865 Frank Calvert, an Englishman whose family had long held lands in the Troad, followed a conjecture about the hill called Hisarlik and discovered the walls of Hellenistic Troy. Heinrich Schliemann then followed, with German money and Teutonic dedication, to tear open the hill, with the results that can be seen today: 'the ruin of a ruin'.

No one who visits Troy (usually called 'Ilium' in Homer) does so because it is the certain birthplace of any real person whose ideas changed the world. But it is, beyond reasonable doubt, the location for the most powerfully told, most influential and most enduring legend the Western world knows: a legend that structured the attitudes and ideals of a civilization for a thousand years.

The book

The Greeks had no Bible or Koran. They had no orthodox, codified religion enforced by state or priest. But they had Homer's *Iliad*, and in a slightly less exalted position the *Odyssey*.

The 15,693 verse lines of the *Iliad* are not a quick read. But they provide an awesome and profoundly moving narrative that opens the door to the whole Classical world. The *Iliad* and the *Odyssey* are the foundation stones of European literature. They are the works that underpin the values of the Classical world in its noonday brightness – a world that lingered to an end in the 4th century of the Christian era. In strange and distorted ways they existed in medieval Europe. Today, their commentary on war and death, and on the destructiveness of human nature, is less known but more needed than ever.

So what are the historical and literary origins of the legend? What is the story? How real are its characters? What are the ideals it contains, which inspired Hellenism and opened the way to the philosophers' questions about life, death and society? It is a long tale: not trivial, not easy, but worth hearing above most others.

Hittites and Mycenaeans

Start by forgetting modern Turkey and modern Greece, with their precise boundaries (established in 1922) and their populations far removed from ancient peoples. There were no Turks in Asia Minor (meaning the geographical area, not the smaller, western part of it that became the Roman province of that name) until after 1016, and none in Constantinople (Istanbul) until 1453. The three ancient areas of influence that need to be understood are Ionia, Anatolia, and the cultural area derived from the place name Mycenae.

Ionia is the eastern coast of the Aegean, the eastern islands – Tenedos, Lesbos, Kos, and the rest – spilling over into the Sea of Marmara (ancient name Propontis) and the coast of south-west Asia Minor. These latter areas are where Greek Ionian settlements or 'colonies' – i.e. towns and cities established by overflow settlers from the older, mother cities – were established from the 7th century BC onwards. The Ionian cities wax and wane (mostly wax until the 4th century AD) while other influences come and go: Persians, Athenian Greeks, Macedonian Greeks under Alexander the Great and his successors, Romans, the decreasingly Roman Byzantines, and finally the Ottoman Turks.

Anatolia is the hinterland of Asia Minor, the vast interior without easy access to coastal trade and influence, and until the nominal control of Alexander, and the more thorough and organized control of the Romans, not Greek at all. The area is of extraordinary antiquity as far as human development is concerned. The archaeologists tell us that there is evidence of human occupation 100,000 years ago. It is the area where wild grasses were first domesticated for use as grain, and emmer, an ancient bearded wheat (not barley), can still be seen growing there. Here, too, goats and sheep were domesticated. But that was time out of mind or record, and what the present visitor can in some measure discern on the ground appeared in about the middle of the second millennium BC, with the Hittite Empire centred on its capital Hattusas, about 130 km (80 miles) east of modern Ankara.

The Hittites were a powerful kingdom of peoples from about 1680 BC. They became more highly organized as an empire, covering all of central Anatolia and northern Syria, from about 1420 BC. They had, and made extensive use of, a written language in cuneiform script. Thousands of tablets have been found in the ruins of Hattusas – international correspondence, word lexicons between different languages, treatises on horse-breeding, instructions for temple rituals and military regulations – and none of them are Greek in any way. Powerful, long-enduring, monarchical, well organized, and highly literate for administrative purposes, the whole Hittite Empire abruptly, and without any known explanation, disappeared in about 1200 BC, within about fifty years of the presumed date of the Trojan War.

Mycenae was a massive and sophisticated citadel or fortress on the crossing point of a number of ancient trade routes on the Greek mainland. It is situated more or less mid-way between Tiryns, at the north end of the Gulf of Argos, and Corinth. It throve between about 1600 and 1200 BC, and gives its name to a characteristic and widely spread culture in which a form of the Greek language – known as Linear B when written – was uniformly used. Bronze was the dominant metal, and the social structure gave rise to the modern label the 'Palace Period'. Places showed a similarity of burial customs, and produced architecture and high-quality artefacts of a similar type. This Mycenaean civilization is evident from sites in the southern half of mainland Greece, and in many of the Aegean islands, including Crete, Rhodes, Samos and Chios. But the Mycenaean culture was not an organized empire in the sense in which Rome and Britain were to have empires. Rather, it was a pattern of life in which the predominant polit-ical structure appears to have been a lord or king in a large fortified palace supported by, regulating, and giving protection to people living within his area of influence. Such organized groupings are best pre-served at Mycenae itself, Tiryns, Pylos and Thebes. It is reasonable to suppose that such similar but independent groups would have cooper-ated for defensive and offensive purposes, as they undoubtedly did for trade and communications.

The Trojan War

If the Trojan War was a real event that happened about 1250 BC – and, legend apart, there is some archaeological and some literary evidence that it *was* a real event and that it happened about this time – it could have been a protracted war of attrition between, on the one hand, a non-Greek power centered at Troy (Ilium, as Homer almost always calls it), which controlled the surrounding area (the Troad) and was an outpost of, or associated with, the Hittite Empire to the east; and, on the other hand, a Mycenaean federation of lords of the Palace Period from mainland Greece.

By a coincidence that has a vaguely sinister feel, something went very wrong with the Mycenaean Greek civilization in the west at about the same time as the disappearance of the Hittite Empire to the east. Whether the collapse in the west was a combination of local Greek civil wars, earthquakes, external (northern?) aggression by 'Dorian' Greeks, or invasion and pillage by the 'boat people' who are mentioned with fear in Egyptian and other records remains unclear. But the outcome was decisive. The palace settlements became villages, the written language disappeared, communications largely ceased, and architecture and crafts degenerated to subsistence levels. It is, however, from this lost land of palaces, great lords and wealth that the Greek lords Achilles, Agamemnon, Menelaus, Odysseus and the rest may well have come. But they reappear after the lapse of five hundred years of unlettered oral transmission, and they are seen through the eyes and language of a new, incipient Greek civilization. Archaic Greece, as it is called to distinguish it from the Classical Greece of the 5th century BC, had a recognizable alphabet drawn from the Phoenician, and produced the literature of Homer and Hesiod, and other, mostly lost, records of legends and stories concerning gods and the Trojan War.

Two questions

In the epic narratives of Homer and others, and in the legends of Troy, we are peering into historical uncertainties of mystifying antiquity and fascination. Two questions are always asked.

The first is how the narratives – particularly the *Iliad* and the Trojan Horse story – relate to real places and real events. Was there a Trojan War? Was Troy finally taken by means of the famous stratagem?

The second question is whether a single man, Homer, wrote the *Iliad* and then the *Odyssey* some time between 750 and 675 BC; whether there were two Homers, one for the *Iliad* and one for the *Odyssey*; or whether these works result from the stitching together at that period of various traditional recitations that were tidied up and edited by later Greek scholars. Did Homer ever exist?

Was there a Trojan War?

A short answer to this question is that there are certain details in the *Iliad* – mainly in Book II – that suggest a Mycenaean or pre-Dark Age origin to the story. Such an origin is arguably consistent with the surviving appearance, and apparent destruction in about 1250 BC, of the walls and towers of what is usually called Troy VI. Indeed, if you stand at the excavated eastern gate of Troy VI, you are probably as close to the death of Hector as time and knowledge will ever permit. The details in the *Iliad* that take us far back in time, perhaps beyond the Dorian Dark Age, include the social structure of kingly leaders and their homes; place names of cities unknown in Classical antiquity but rediscovered by modern archaeologists; the high value always put upon bronze (not the later iron) armour; the descriptions of certain artefacts that match archaeological finds (such as the famous boar-tusk helmet found at Knossos and exactly described in the *Iliad*, X.260–65); and the topography of the Troad.

The Troad comprises the large area of land south of Troy, including the range of hills centred on Mount Ida and the river system of the Scamander and the Simoeis, and the plain of Troy to the north and north-west of the city. But to make sense of the position of the Greek fleet and fighting as described by Homer, it has to be understood that a large part of what is now flat agricultural land to the north was then a bay of the sea accessible from the Hellespont and separated from the Aegean by the Sigeum Ridge. Once we understand this, much of Homer's narrative fits the topography.

But in tracing the source of the Trojan War legends to a real conflict in about 1250 BC between (maybe) Mycenaean Greeks and (maybe) a powerful outpost of the Hittite Empire, it cannot be emphasized strongly enough that the eventual written narrative was constructed after the vagaries of about five hundred years of oral, bardic transmission and elaboration, during which time the stability of written records did not exist. In the *Iliad* there is only one reference to writing, and the reference makes it clear that writing is suspect, if not as a black art, then certainly as a means of causing secret mischief. King Proteus, wishing to kill Bellerophon but lacking confidence to do so himself, sent him into Lycia and gave him 'fatal tokens, scratching in a folded tablet signs many and deadly, and ordered him to show them to his father-in-law, so that he might perish'.

So was there some real, if remote, historical conflict in which the Trojan War legends had their origin? Very probably, yes. Was the transmission of these legends over a period of five hundred years written or oral? Oral. How, then, did the vast and wonderful works of literature always attributed to Homer come into being?

Did Homer exist?

It has sometimes been asked whether there was ever a single man called 'Homer' who put the two epics together. Perhaps there were two Homers: a younger and more vigorous man, acutely aware of human passions and conflicts, who wrote the *Iliad*; and another man, older, more world-weary and in search of a domestic resolution of conflict at the end of life, who wrote the *Odyssey*.

Apart from the near absence of any such 'two Homers' tradition in antiquity, it seems to be stretching literary credulity beyond even its imaginative limits to suppose that, at the very beginning of European writing – out of nothing, as it were – not just one but two writers of the highest genius suddenly appeared. If one has to account for the different linguistic and emotional tone of the two books and the more 'archaic' feel of the *Iliad*, why not say that the *Iliad* was constructed by a man in the fullness of life and the *Odyssey* by the same man many years later, reflecting on life's journey?

Another suggestion is that 'Homer' was merely a scribe, or chief of a group of scribes, who exercised their collective efforts to gather together various orally transmitted stories and to make them into a continuous tale – a late grubbing together of two sets of traditional narratives. The trouble here – apart, again, from the general ancient attribution of the stories to a single man – is that it beggars belief that anything so vast, so closely knit, so well ordered, complex, emotionally profound and consistent, could have been just cobbled together. It is certainly true that both texts have been tidied up – initially for recitation in Athens in the period 550–530 BC, and more thoroughly by scholars in the library of Alexandria in the 3rd century BC – but even the most fastidious editing does not create works of genius any more than textual annotation can make the plays of Shakespeare great.

So the most plausible answer to the questions about authorship is that the two epics were constructed by one man: the earlier and longer *Iliad* (15,693 lines of verse; compare Milton's *Paradise Lost*, which has a mere 10,365 lines) perhaps in Homer's early manhood; and the *Odyssey* (at 12,110 lines) in his old age, both works drawing upon oral tradition.

The narratives

The *Iliad* is a detailed account of certain events towards the end of a ten-year war in which a confederation of Greeks, or 'Argives' or 'Achaeans', attack Troy/Ilium and its allies, the 'Danaans'. It tells of the folly of anger and pride, and of the pity of war. Agamemnon, the Greek leader, angers Achilles, the Greeks' most ferocious fighter, by unjustly claiming from him a prize of war. In anger, Achilles withdraws from the fighting, taking his followers – the Myrmidons – with him. The Trojan prince Hector leads an attack on the Greek ships drawn up on the shore, and the Greeks, badly led by Agamemnon, are all but overwhelmed. Achilles refuses to assist but sends his closest friend, Patroclus, to fight in his stead. Patroclus is killed by Hector. Achilles is consumed with grief and anger over what has happened, and sets out to kill Hector. Hector, warned that he cannot win, fails to make any convincing effort to escape Achilles and is killed, whereupon Achilles dishonours the body by dragging it around Troy behind his chariot. All this takes place in just two days of fighting separated by two days of truce, and is recounted in the first twenty-two books of the *Iliad*. The last events are narrated in Books XXIII and XXIV, and cover a period of about thirteen days. They record the strange meeting in the Greek camp at night between Achilles and Priam, the aged king of Troy and Hector's father, and the giving back of Hector's body to Priam for performance of the funeral rites – the gods having been so offended by Achilles' unseemly behaviour that they have kept the body undecayed and beautiful. 'Thus they performed the funeral rites of Hector, tamer of horses', are the final words of the epic.

The *Odyssey* has a much more complex literary structure, with time shifts and a narrative spread over many years. It contains the famous stories of the Cyclops, the Sirens, the Lotus-Eaters, the descent into the House of Hades, the first recorded reference to Troy captured through the device of the Wooden Horse, and much more – all embedded within the story of Telemachus, Odysseus' son, setting out from Ithaca to find his father as his mother's suitors prepare to kill him. The second half of the story recounts Odysseus' secret return to Ithaca and his reunion with Penelope after the killing of the rapacious suitors. The epic ends: '"Odysseus of many devices, now hold your hand, now halt the strife of endless war lest Zeus be offended." So spoke Athene, and he obeyed, and was glad at heart.'

From the same period (*c.* 750–675 BC) there survive a number of fragmentary or summary items known as the 'Epic Cycle', which give some account of events that took place before the war, such as the Judgment of Paris, and of events that happened between the death of Hector and the final dispersal of the Greek forces. They include the story of the death of Achilles, shot in the heel by Paris, Hector's brother, and the universally known stratagem of the Wooden Horse – later retold by Virgil, greatest of Roman poets, in Book II of the *Aeneid*. There were other very ancient accounts of the war, or parts of it, but they appear to have perished even before the 5th century BC.

Caution: hard read ahead
Not only the few school children who still battle with the original Greek, but also the mature reader confronting the best translations

will find difficulties in getting through the *Iliad*. Why? To appreciate in advance the obstacles is in part to overcome them; to overcome them is to enter into the world of perhaps the greatest book ever written. In no particular order, but from my own experience, some of the difficulties are these:

❖ The medium of verse narrative is strange to us, who seldom read Milton, and Sir Walter Scott scarcely at all. When combined with the difficulties of rendering ancient Greek into English, it tends to result in a lumpy and uncomfortable word order that no translator who tries to keep close to the original meaning can ever entirely overcome, although some, notably Robert Fitzgerald (in the Oxford World's Classics series), do very well.

❖ There are a number of bardic repeats in the text – descriptive choruses or reiterated messages that served to give the oral narrator a rest. These are omitted in some translations. But other idiosyncrasies cannot be brushed out without altering the whole feel of the work. These include the recurring epithet: 'the resourceful Odysseus', 'the ruffian god' (Ares), 'the black ships', and so on. In addition there are the names or epithets that vary according to the scansion of the verse, but not according to the needs of the story: 'Pallas' is often swapped with 'Athene', for example, and we read of 'the swift ships' even when the ships in question are beached. But if these consequences of the verse form make our reading more difficult, why did they not cause problems for the original hearers? To explain briefly: in almost all early storytelling, the medium was verse – it 'sings' better than prose; it is easier to remember; and its familiar refrains and established word repeats help to carry both bard and audience over what to us, exhausted by more than a few minutes of concentrated listening, would be intolerable periods. Thus it was that, for the purpose of storytelling, verse came before prose in almost all societies.

❖ Another difficulty is the intrusion into the story of other beings – the gods – in whom we simply do not believe, and whose activity looks like a cheat in the narrative. But when a god is said to intrude upon human affairs, what happens can very often be seen as unexpected good or bad luck, and undoubtedly some of Homer's Classical readers read it in this way. (More of this anon.)

❖ An early block to reading the *Iliad* is the second half of Book II. Having got off to a splendid start with the quarrel between Agamemnon and Achilles, and the resulting council held by the Greek chiefs, the story halts for what feels like an interminable list of participants in the war – Greek and Trojan – and the places they come from. The archaeologist and scholar will linger; the reader will probably want to resume at Book III. If the funeral rites of Patroclus produce a similar response, a similar solution is at hand!

❖ There is an enormous and exhausting proliferation of largely unfamiliar person and place names in the *Iliad*: about 750 in all. Just read over them. The story depends on about eighteen named humans and about twelve gods. Get to know them and their relationships. The effort will be no greater than that required by a newcomer to a radio or television soap opera, and just possibly of more enduring value.

Real people or vacuous heroes?

The immortals in the *Iliad* obviously have individual characters, but are the mortals any more than heroic cyphers to whom are attributed deeds of valour, cowardice, anger, folly, honour or dishonour? If sometimes they are heroic cyphers, they are also, I believe, distinct and realistic human individuals. Look at some of the Greeks:

Agamemnon, commander-in-chief, is domineering, arrogant, and a bad judge of men and of himself. Note how, at the start, when attempting to shame the Greeks into fighting by saying that they had better pack up and go home, he is all but taken at his word. He is too easily wrong-footed by situations. He is proud, dictatorial and, under pressure, indecisive.

Ajax, son of Telemon (there are two Ajaxes), is an impetuous, muscle-bound thug, insensitive, brave, brutal and stupid – the perfect archetype of the action-movie 'hero'.

Achilles is a passionate man, too easily moved to destructive anger. His row with Agamemnon indirectly causes the death of his beloved friend Patroclus. He over-reacts to this misfortune, not only killing Hector but dishonouring his body – and therefore himself – in the process. Achilles is darkly resigned to his own death. He is portrayed as a great but flawed human being: violent, brave, proud, and in the end redeemed by sorrow shared with the man whose son he has killed – a frightening and complex man.

Nestor is old, experienced, wise, garrulous and opinionated, whether circumstances are appropriate or not – the very epitome of the semi-retired leader who commands deference and sometimes earns it.

Patroclus is young, gentle to women and to his friends, brave, but in the end too brave to survive.

However, it is the three main Trojan characters who seem to stand out most clearly as human personalities:

Priam, king of Troy, is old and weary of war, suffering endless loss and an ever increasing ruin that he half knows will lead to the destruction of everything that is his – the death of his sons, the enslavement of his daughter Cassandra and of his family, and his own death. He is a man of sorrows fated to failure, left pleading for the body of his dead son.

Paris (also called Alexandros) – the human cause of the whole mess – is 'vivid and beautiful', elegant, a delightful lover, brave and effective up to a point, and clever. He eventually kills Achilles by means of a trick, but he is never quite where he should be at the crucial moment. At one stage Hector finds him 'cheering on his company'. Reprimanded, Paris replies:

We are behind you, we are fresh
And lack no spirit in attack, I promise,
Up to the limit of our strength.
Beyond that no man fights though he may wish it.
(XIII.784–87)

Earlier in the fighting Paris had been 'slow to leave the place where he had discoursed with his lady', and when he eventually turns up, he says to his brother Hector, 'Dear fellow, have I kept you waiting? Have I not come at the right time as you asked?' Hector's reply is worth quoting for its humanity and for its implied longing for the cessation of war – a longing that permeates this most war-centred of all stories:

And Hector in his shimmering helm replied:
'My strange brother! No man with justice in him
Would underrate your handiwork in battle;
You have a powerful arm. But you give way
Too easily, and lose interest, lose your will.
My heart aches in me when I hear our men,
Who have such toil of battle on your account,
Talk of you with contempt. Well, come along.
Some day we'll make amends for that, if ever
We drive the Achaeans from the land of Troy –
If ever Zeus permit us, in our hall,
To set before the gods of heaven, undying
And ever young, our wine bowl of deliverance. (VI.520–end)

But of course they never will. Within two days Hector will be dead. The proud counterpart of Achilles, who is portrayed without the vice of anger, and, at home in Troy, as loving to his wife and tender to his baby son, binds himself to fight against the impossible odds of Achilles. Of his character it is best you form your own opinion. You may even conclude that he is the real hero of the *Iliad*.

2

Troy: The Book and the Ideals

To know what Homer wrote is to know at source the values and ideas that underpinned the Hellenic world in particular and the Classical world in general for a thousand years. In this way he is the ultimate source for the ideas of the philosophers concerning war, death, luck, the gods, and certain norms of personal character. Through them, what Homer has to say touches not only Classical history, but us.

War, anger and courage

The first – unexpected – point to note about the *Iliad* is that, although the whole epic is concerned with the Trojan War, war is never treated as a good thing, as a state of affairs justified by the virtues it draws out of men – virtues like courage, self-sacrifice and comradeship. Ares, the god of war – Mars to the Romans – is not sacrificed to, prayed to or praised. He is 'the ruffian god', the 'bane of mankind', 'crusted with blood', 'man-destroying'. And war itself is condemned by the wise:

> Merops Percosius, the seer,
> Profoundest of all seers, had refused
> To let his sons take the path of war –
> Man-wasting war – but they were heedless of him,
> Driven on by dark powers of death. (II.828–33)

Earlier in Book II, 'Both sides hoped for an end of miserable war', and later, when there was some hope of peace, both sides 'held up their hands to heaven'. (The Greeks prayed standing up and looking up, not grovelling on their knees as Eastern kings and gods demanded.) They prayed: 'Father Zeus, almighty over Ida, most glorious, most grand, let us be loyal friends in peace.' But once 'the dogs of war', 'the shameless butchery of war' are let loose, anger and violence run free: 'In one same air elation and agony of men destroying and destroyed.'

It is not war, but one of its causes and accompaniments, that generates the *Iliad*. The very first line tells all: 'Anger be now our song, immortal one'. It is not merely Achilles' anger, which is directed at Agamemnon, but also Agamemnon's anger at Achilles, Menelaus' anger at Helen and Paris, the gods Athene and Hera's anger at Paris and the Trojans as a whole, and the anger that fighting lets loose and enflames. And of course anger is an actual aid to victory on the battlefield. Provoke a man to enough anger and he is almost invincible at that moment. And one way to provoke such anger on the battlefield is to accuse a man of cowardice – a shameful thing in Homer's world.

So the dreadful consequences of anger, of the wild and uncontrolled anger that harms individuals, gods and nations, are worked out in the *Iliad*. This concern manifests itself again in later philosophical thinking, such as the Socratic appeal for self-control, knowing yourself, doing nothing to excess, not rushing upon destruction by the route of unbridled passion. The caveats are already writ large in Homer: 'We learned from old stories how towering wrath could overcome great men'; and again: 'Folly is strong and swift, outrunning all the prayers, and everywhere arriving first to injure mortal men.' Clearest of all is this warning: 'Control your passion, and your proud heart, for gentle courtesy is a better thing.' These quotations are from Book IX, but they are typical of the *Iliad* as a whole.

Even in war, even in the heroic war of the *Iliad*, courage does not mean rushing into certain death. Agamemnon beseeches his brother Menelaus not to fight Hector: 'Give up this wish for emulation's sake to face a stronger fighter.' And Paris is just in promising to fight 'up to the limits of our strength. Beyond that no man fights.' Patroclus dies unnecessarily because he disregards this care; and so does Hector: 'Unmoved Hector the prince stood at the gates of Troy, resolute to fight Achilles'. His father pleads: 'He is more powerful than you by far, and pitiless: come into Troy ...' (XXII.33–40). But he does not, and dies, in the end wonderfully, but inopportunely brave.

Death and an afterlife

The *Iliad* is full of death and killing, but there is nothing, absolutely nothing, heroic, desirable or rewarding in being dead. Martyrdom has no reward. Violent death is precisely and relentlessly described many times, but it is never the simple falling over of a bloodless man of straw that we see so often on television and in films, where death is trivialized and made small for entertainment. Death is always powerful, and dreadful, and final, and the description almost always ends with the grim acknowledgment that 'darkness veiled his eyes', or with references to 'numbing darkness' or 'fateful darkness', or to the fallen man entering 'the unending night of death'. Death ends everything a man is. It is the brother of sleep, but for ever, and it is never to be chosen ('better a living dog than a dead hero'). Even heroic Achilles acknowledges:

> Now I think
> No riches can compare with being alive …
> A man may come by cattle and sheep in raids;
> Tripods he buys, and tawny-headed horses.
> But his life's breath cannot be hunted back
> Or be recaptured once it pass his lips. (IX.406–9)

The melancholy of human brevity and of our end is everywhere in the *Iliad*, and echoes down the centuries from it in one of the most memorable, and remembered, of its many extended similes:

> Like leaves upon the earth are
> The generations of men – old leaves, cast
> On the ground by wind, young leaves the
> Greening forest bears when spring comes in.
> So mortals pass; one generation flowers
> Even as another dies away. (VI.145–49; see also XXI.426–67)

These sentiments were echoed by the Athenian playwright Aristophanes three hundred years later, in the *The Birds*: 'Consider the generations of men who perish and fade as leaves … frail castings of clay.' And again Virgil, greatest of Roman poets, seven hundred years after Homer, in Book VI of the *Aeneid*, in a wonderful evocation of the universality of departing life:

> Dense as the leaves that from the trees
> Float down when autumn first is keen,

Or as the birds that thickly massed
Fly landward from the ocean vast
Driven over seas by wintery blast
To seek a sunnier sky,
So each in pathetic suppliance stands
And stretches out their eager hands
In yearning for the farther shore.

These are the newly dead, but the shore for which they yearn is beyond
Lethe, the river of oblivion, and that is Homer's message: death is the
darkening of the eyes, nothingness. At most, and perhaps worst, it is a
period of grey, dreamlike waiting before proper burial of the body gives
rest for ever. This is the matter of Achilles' dream about Patroclus
(Book XXIII), in which he acknowledges that a 'wisp of life remains in
the undergloom of death'. But that is before the river is crossed.

Let me call this long-ago view of death the 'natural account'. It is
natural because it adds nothing to what death looks like equally in a
dog, a fly or a man: the end. The wise man avoids it as long as honour
and practicalities allow, but when it comes, as the English playwright
John Drinkwater was to write two-and-a-half thousand years after
Homer, 'The bearing of man facing it is all.' Hector, about to be killed,
speaks thus:

It is finished … Death is near, and black,
Not at a distance, not to be avoided …
Still I would not die without delivering
A stroke … but in some action memorable
To men in days to come … (XXII.295–305)

The view of death that expects no afterlife worth having was widespread in early Classical antiquity, but there was never a single, agreed
or orthodox expectation that most people were expected to share,
whether philosophical or religious. Among the philosophers, Socrates
and Plato developed complex and highly sophisticated arguments for
the immortality of the soul. These were in turn to become part of the
metaphysical structure of Christian theology. On the other hand
Aristotle, and more emphatically the Atomists (Democritus and

Epicurus) produced powerful arguments and evidence for the soul's mortality, in the sense that they regarded it either as part of the body, like the brain, or as a function of the living body, one of its activities. This conclusion looks akin to what we might now regard as the 'scientific' rather than the 'religious' attitude to death. But of all this more in later chapters.

When the ancient mystery cults tried to give form to some alternative to Homer's darkness of death, they seem to have been vague, confused and contrary. Orphism and the Dionysiac rituals appear to involve a two-world structure in which life moves on from one world to another. The Pythagoreans believed that at the moment of death the soul moved on into some new bodily incarnation in this world. The Eleusinian mysteries seem to have presupposed some sort of beatific existence. But in all cases the sources are either confused or lost. What is not in dispute is that beliefs about what to expect at death were varied, conflicting, changing with time and place, and never codified in any agreed formula. But Homer did provide one commanding picture.

Even in Homer there is another suggestion. In a few lines in the *Odyssey*, Proteus of Egypt, 'the ancient sea god', tells Menelaus that he will not meet his end 'in the grazing-land of horses in Argos': 'The deathless ones will waft you to the world's end, the Elysian fields where yellow-haired Rhadamanthus is.' Why? Because Menelaus is married to, united with, Helen, whose father is Zeus. Menelaus has a kind of deathlessness by association with a deathless one. The majority of us are less fortunate.

The other, longer, encounter with the dead occurs in Book XI of the *Odyssey*. Odysseus goes down into the Underworld – the House of Hades – and converses with the hapless dead; but they have forgotten. They are 'the unknowing' until they drink the dark blood Odysseus has brought with him and briefly remember themselves. But this afterlife is scarcely life at all. It is a dim, confused, shadowy existence; mostly a forgetting, and certainly not an existence worth looking forward to from any real, full-blooded life, however poor that life may be.

In sum: Homer provides a sharp distinction between mortals who die and the immortal gods – in other respects quite like human beings – who do not. For mortals, there is either nothing at death – the dead person is no more than the naturally decomposing body – or, at most, there may be a ghostly lingering before the funeral rites allow the person to cross the waters of oblivion. Beyond that is the House of Hades, the place for those who have forgotten themselves – dark, meaningless, and unattractive from the point of view of everything that made life worth having. For a very select few, through their association with the deathless ones, there is Elysium.

Gods and luck

Men are mortal, were born and will die. Only gods are immortal, but not even they are eternal. What is eternal never came into existence and will never go out of existence. But in some way the gods were 'born'. They came into existence as part of the natural universe, but they will not go out of existence, and they interfere in human affairs. They are, moreover, not moral archetypes. They are like a big, powerful, partly democratic, sometimes quarrelsome, generally happy human family. They disagree about whom to support in war, and they actively intervene to save a fighter or to change the course of a battle.

If you don't like this notion of anthropomorphic gods, if it seems contrived or primitive, think of them, as Homer almost suggests on occasions, as the causes of the wise or foolish decisions we sometimes make without good reason, or as luck as it applies to natural events: the mist that suddenly drifts over a battlefield, allowing a hero in danger to escape, or the river that abruptly floods, thus preventing an advance or retreat. And 'luck' or 'a god' can become our destiny – the invisible, apparently random influences that bring us good things or bad, death or life. One response to such luck is a fatalistic acceptance of whatever happens, the Islamic 'will of Allah'. Another is making the best we can of unavoidable outcomes, and adjusting our responses to them: the Stoic way. A third is the Homeric approach: to try to propitiate the gods – since they can, to a certain extent, be influenced by appropriate attention to sacrifice and forms of respect – but always to accept what they give.

So it is that Achilles warns men to 'Honour the gods' will. They may honour ours.' Paris, too, claims that 'Glorious things the gods bestow are not to be despised, being as the gods will. Wishing will not bring them.' And Nestor affirms: 'The immortal gods have given men all things in season.' Perhaps the most illuminating comment of all occurs when a Greek fighter aims an arrow at Hector, but the string of his bow snaps: 'Damn the luck. Some god is cutting off our prospects in this fight.' His friend Ajax responds by telling him to pick up a shield and spear and get on with it as best he can.

Most famously, the conditions of luck or fortune are described by Achilles in his night encounter with Priam:

> Come … let us sit down.
> We'll probe our wounds no more but let them rest,
> Though grief lies heavy on us. Tears heal nothing,
> Drying so stiff and cold. This is the way
> The gods ordained the destiny of men,
> To bear such burdens in our lives, while they
> Feel no affliction. At the door of Zeus
> Are those two urns of good and evil gifts
> That he may choose for us; and one for whom
> The lightning's king dips in both urns
> Will have by turns bad luck and good. But one
> To whom he sends all evil … that man goes
> Contemptible by the will of Zeus. (XXIV.522–33)

The same idea occurs more simply in the *Odyssey*: 'It is Zeus himself who from Olympus allots prosperity among men – gives to the good or the bad, to every one of them as he pleases' (VI.186–90).

So for the heroes of the *Iliad* and the *Odyssey* (and, via them, for all the literate Classical world – no tiny number), there is a certain partial randomness in human affairs – 'luck', or the obscure activity of human-like agents called gods. The gods may hear our wishes, and act for us if we give them 'their due'. But they may not hear us, or may choose not to act for us, or some other god may get in the way. In all cases we must do what we can and endure: 'The bearing of man facing it is all.'

Character and conduct

What should the bearing of man be? Classical writers – Greek and Roman – for a thousand years and more after Homer looked to his works for examples or aphoristic justification for what they did or urged to be done. If an example could be found in Homer, it had author-ity. It commended your case. There are hundreds of such references in

Plato (427–347 BC) and Plutarch (*c.* AD 46–*c.* 120), and scores in Lucian (*c.* AD 115–after 180), Athenaeus (flourished around AD 200) and in most other literary sources – including, at the end, Julianus (emperor of Rome; ruled AD 360–63), Macrobius (flourished about AD 400; 'the last testament of civilized Hellenism') and Boethius (AD 476–524; 'the last of the Romans').

For a world created by Christianity and Islam, the question: 'What should I do?' would be answered in a very general way by the response: 'The will of God'. It is thus somewhat disconcerting to find no such general answer in Classical antiquity. Zeus and his company had great, though not infinite, powers, but they neither exemplify nor – except in the grossest cases – demand moral rectitude in any sense we would recognize. Civic arrangements were governed by political constitutions and accepted custom. For Plato and the Stoics, and more emphatically for Aristotle and the Epicureans, ethics are about personal character and the happy life. Likewise at source – that is, in Homer – what is valued or condemned is centred on human character in relation to other people. So what are Homeric ethics? (The word is anachronistic in referring to so early a period, but let it suffice.)

❖ Anger must be held in check except in battle.

❖ Bravery is admirable within realistic limits.

❖ Pride is destructive. Thus Patroclus rebukes Achilles: 'You and your fearsome pride! What good will come of it to anyone, later, unless you keep disaster from the Argives? Have you no pity?'

❖ Respect for the dead is important. Achilles fails in this, declaring that he will let Hector's body be eaten by wild dogs. But the gods Aphrodite and Apollo intervene to prevent such an outrage.

❖ Honour friendship and family ties, even when you find yourself fighting on different sides. Thus Diomedes 'smiled at the young [Trojan] captain, saying gently, "Why, you are my friend! My grandfather, Oeneus, made friends of us long ago ... So let us keep from one another's weapons in the spear-fights of this war.

Trojans a-plenty will be left for me ... and many Achaeans will be left for you to bring down if you can".'

❖ Mercy and pity are commendable and can be bought. (Compare modern Islam, where a penalty paid by the aggressor can cancel the hurt.) For example, in Homer: 'There is no pity in him. A normal man will take the penalty for a brother slain or a dead son. By paying much, the one who did the deed may stay unharmed at home.'

❖ Sympathy is possible and to be commended. '"Now must I mourn your death for ever, who were for ever gentle." She wept again, and women sobbed about her, first for Patroclus, then for each other's grief.'

❖ Luxury is not a corrupting concern of heroes. Luxuries are objects of wonder, but chieftains are accustomed to practical everyday work with their own hands.

❖ Good marriage receives a touching and unexpected tribute in Homer: witness Hector and Andromache in the *Iliad*, and Odysseus and Penelope in the *Odyssey*.

❖ Freedom is longed for, but it is freedom from killing, slavery and war – not freedom to do what one wants.

❖ Justice – of a sort – is valued. Even Zeus in the here and now punishes 'men who use violence and give crooked rulings in public places of assembly and drive justice out.'

❖ Charity has a value. Even as late as AD 362, the emperor Julianus, seeking to show that Christians did not have a monopoly of charity to the poor or to the alien, quotes from the *Odyssey*: 'Now it falls to us to tend him, for Zeus is patron of every stranger and every beggar, and to such as these, even a humble gift means much' (VI.204–9). And again: 'Stranger, it is not right for me to slight a stranger even though one of less account than you were to come. For all strangers and beggars are from Zeus, and a gift, though small, is welcome from such as us.' (The speaker is a poor man.) (XIV.56–61)

Finally, men of old were stronger and more heroic than the present generation and to be remembered, for honourable death or victory in battle *is* greatness. A man is, and is remembered, for what he has achieved, and *that is all he is or will ever be.* Challenging an Achaean to fight with him, Hector speaks thus:

> One day a man on shipboard, sailing by
> On the wine-dark sea, will point landward and say:
> 'There is the death mound of an ancient man,
> A hero who fought Hector and was slain.'
> Someone will say that one day. And the honour
> Won by me here will never pass away. (VII.87–91)

When you sail north or south, going to or from the Hellespont on the Aegean, look east, at the Sigeum Ridge that divides the plain of Troy from the Aegean. There you will see the death mound of an ancient man and be close to Hector: as close in the pity of war as the Greeks and Trojans are to the thousands of Turks and Allied soldiers who lie buried to the north of the Hellespont, with their memorials to the carnage of Gallipoli.

* * *

Nothing substitutes for Homer himself: the *Iliad* in Robert Fitzgerald's translation (Oxford, 1998), and the *Odyssey,* perhaps in T. E. Lawrence's translation (New York, 1932) or in the translation by Robert Fagles for Penguin Classics (Harmondsworth, new edn 1992). The ancient topography of Troy has been beautifully described and illustrated by J. V. Luce in *Celebrating Homer's Landscapes* (New Haven, Conn., 1998). The origins and progress of the Trojan War, in as far as they can be ascertained, are given in Barry Strauss, *The Trojan War: A New History* (New York, 2006) and Michael Wood, *In Search of the Trojan War* (London, 1985; revd edn 2005). Both are well illustrated and easily read.

3

Miletus:
The Nature of the Universe

Miletus has a stronger claim than any other place on earth to be the primary source of all enquiries about the physical composition and structure of the universe. These unprecedented speculations, which set in train a process towards whose end we hurtle ever faster, are always associated with three names from the period of the city's greatness, before the coming of the Persian in 546 BC. They are the long-lived Thales, who was born well before 585 BC but probably flourished for the next forty years or so; Anaximander, who was Thales' younger contemporary but is likely to have died about the same time as him; and Anaximenes, a relatively minor figure who was born about 585 and lived for sixty years or more.

These names were known and revered throughout antiquity, but their works – and we only know for certain that one of them, Anaximander, wrote a book – are lost. They are known to us by ancient tradition; by the comments of Aristotle two hundred years later; by anecdote and summary, particularly in the sometimes reliable and always garrulous *Lives of the Philosophers* by one Diogenes Laertius, who wrote around AD 210; and by a quotation in Simplicus – a learned commentator on Aristotle who had the sad distinction of being one of the philosophers expelled from Athens in AD 529 by Justinian when he put a forceful end to all intellectual alternatives to Christianity. But despite the fragments of darkened glass in which we have to try to see the Milesians, something of them can be discerned, if only in the ideas that enduring tradition always attributed to them.

Thales
Lists of the seven sages of antiquity vary, but they always include Thales. He was renowned as an astute politician and sagacious citizen,

an astronomer, a mathematician, and a 'physicalist' – one who tries to understand the workings of nature (close to our word 'physicist').

As with Sir Winston Churchill or Sir Thomas Beecham, one suspects that Thales, truly a remarkable human being in his own right, was also a convenient peg on which to hang good anecdotes or quotations. Three from Diogenes Laertius give their flavour:

> In answer to the question what was the rarest thing he had ever seen, he replied 'An aged tyrant'.

> On being asked what is difficult, he replied. 'To know oneself.' What is easy? 'To advise other people.' What is pleasant? 'Success.'

> The story is told that, when his mother urged him to marry, he replied it was too soon, and when she pressed him again later in life, he replied it was too late.

Plato, in the *Theaetetus*, succinctly portrays him as the typical philosopher who knows 'the essence of man' but is 'unacquainted with his next-door neighbour': 'He was examining the stars and gazing at the sky when he fell into a well. A clever and witty Thracian servant girl remarked that he was so concerned with what was going on in the heavens that he couldn't see in front of his own feet.'

In contrast, other stories attribute to him the practical wisdom of making a lot of money by hiring at a low cost all the olive presses in a year when he foresaw a bumper crop, and the political acumen of ensuring that Miletus avoided a fatal conflict with the Persians by not giving Croesus any support when he was fighting them (Croesus lost). Aristotle reports the story about the olive presses in the *Politics*, commenting astringently that this does not show any particular wisdom in Thales: 'The device of taking an opportunity to secure a monopoly is a universal principle of business.'

The best-attested of Thales' practical achievements occurred on 28 May 585 BC. He had predicted a total eclipse of the sun for that date: as Herodotus reports, the eclipse duly occurred as a battle between the Medes and the Lydians was taking place: 'The day was suddenly

Thales observing the stars – and about to fall into a well.

Thales footling with his distance calculator.

turned into night … as a consequence they ceased from fighting and became anxious to make peace.' How did he make the prediction? It can only have been through a combination of knowledge of Babylonian and Egyptian astronomical records, and luck. Ancient Babylonian records had established that eclipses occur every 223 lunar months (the so-called 'Saros cycle'). If Thales had seen or heard of the eclipse that was visible in Egypt in 603, he would have expected an eclipse to occur somewhere in 585; the luck was in its being visible in the right place, and at a significant moment.

As an astronomer and meteorologist, Thales was reputed to have shown that one year contained 365 days, to have calculated the dates of the winter and summer solstices, and to have estimated the sizes of the sun and moon.

The most famous Hellenic geometer, Euclid, was comparatively late, living very approximately 325–250 BC. But among the earliest figures Thales had a high reputation. When one looks at his reputed achievements, they appear to have practical application rather than to be the systematic proofs and demonstrations typical of later Greek geometry. For example, he calculated the height of the pyramids by measuring the length of their shadows at the time of day when the shadow of a man was the same as his height. He constructed a simple device for measuring the distance of a ship from the shore (important to know if it had hostile intent!): get a straight stick with a crosspiece fastened near its top that can be directed downwards at an angle. Fix the stick upright on the top of a tower, hill or high building, and tilt the crosspiece so that it is pointing directly at the ship. Leaving the crosspiece at the same angle, twist the stick round until the crosspiece is pointing at some object on low land whose distance from the tower or hill is known. The distance of the ship in practical terms is about the same. A final example of Thales' geometry is not the proof but the practical utility of a geometrical construction for establishing a right angle – so important in building. Construct a circle (easily done) and bisect it through its centre with a straight line. A right angle will then be established at any point on the circumference where straight lines from the extremities of the diameter are constructed to meet.

Thales as physicalist

In what we would call the beginnings of natural science, Thales' reputation as the first contributor to any rationally grounded account of the
physical world depends upon three proposals that were always attributed to him.

The first is that the basic stuff of all things is water. Why water?
Perhaps because water exists as a solid, a liquid and a gas; or because it
is not obvious that water comes from anything other than itself; or
because Thales observed that life is found very commonly and cannot
exist without water. A further reason (note, a reason, however mis-
guided – not a belief or myth) was his second proposal: that the whole
earth floats on water. A rational explanation for earthquakes would
then be the earth rocking, like a boat, on its watery bed. As so often,
Aristotle, with lofty intelligence and two hundred years later, can
dismiss such odd suggestions at a stroke:

> Thales supposes that the earth is at rest because it can float
> like wood or similar substances ... But this is to forget that
> the same may be said of the water supporting the earth as
> was said of the earth itself. It is not in the nature of water,
> any more than of earth, to remain suspended. It rests on
> something. (*On the Heavens*, II)

It may be that the idea of the earth resting on water came to Thales
from Egyptian, Babylonian and Jewish religious myths, of the sort
familiar from the Bible: 'In the beginning ... darkness was upon the
face of the deep, and the spirit of God was moving upon the face of the
waters'. But the difference is that Thales' suggestion was evidently not
propounded by him as part of any dogmatic truth. In his own lifetime
Anaximander had a better account of how the earth rested in space;
Anaximenes had proposed a fundamentally different stuff – air – as the
source of all things; and Thales lived long enough, and in an intimate
enough city, to have known about and discussed these alternatives.

Thales' third suggestion about the physical world sounds even
more odd to us. It is that, in simplistic translation, 'a magnet has a soul'.
This is not as absurd as it sounds. The word conventionally translated
as 'soul' is *psuche*. Its force differs according to the arguments of the

later philosophers who use it – Plato, Aristotle, Epicurus and others – but, originally, to have a *psuche* was to be *empsuchos,* to be animate or living; and one of the characteristics of what lives is its ability to cause movement in other things or in itself. A magnet (or lodestone) can do just this. It is therefore a form of life – a mistaken conclusion, but not an arbitrary or irrational one.

The nature of the universe

The ancient Greek word *phusis* means 'nature', and includes everything except artefacts and the results of human activity. So if someone wrote a book 'On Nature', as Anaximander did, it would be an enquiry into the physical structure or workings of what we call the natural world. In that sense Thales' suggestion that water is the basic stuff of everything is the first non-religious, non-mythological attempt to probe beneath the multifarious appearances of things to seek a common generator. Anaximenes' alternative – air – is different, but it answers the same new question.

To us, both answers are silly, but to think the question is the colossal achievement. Why should it ever be asked? Isn't it obvious that there are thousands of different things made from a wide range of stuffs? Of course it is obvious! So obvious that the unobvious question – about the possibility of a basic stuff common to everything – had never been asked. And if the unobvious question had remained unasked, there would be no chemistry or physics now. And Thales asked the unobvious question.

The Jewish god was – is – awesome, invisible, the eternal creator, the reason why all is as it is. But belief in such a god tells you nothing about how things work, what they are made of, or how the creator has structured the universe in which we have to find our way. In the beginning, the majesty of god closes questions.

The pagan gods (whose relationships and activities are described by Hesiod, a near contemporary of Homer, in a surviving work called the *Theogony*) explain natural happenings in terms of animistic myths, so that – to take one example – spring is the return of a goddess from the underworld. This, too, pre-empts the questions of natural science, but less comprehensively than Jehovah. For the pagan, there is no fixed canon of stories that have to be believed. More significantly, Hesiod's gods are not responsible for the universe as a whole. They did not create it. They even fear 'the dark limits of the barren sea and the starry sky', and it is these that the speculative daring of the Milesians began to plumb with questions no man had been known to ask before. What is it made of? How does it work? Where does it come from? How did living creatures come into being? Within 150 years, this series of questions would lead to the astounding answer we still depend upon today: the ancient atomic theory.

Anaximander

With Anaximander, there is a further and profoundly original move in the Milesian attempts to understand nature. His suggestion is that what we have now, the world as a whole and all the things that compose it, formed (without the intervention of gods) out of a pre-existing, inanimate infinity. To refer to this state Anaximander created from ordinary language the first abstract scientific term in the known history of thought: *to apeiron*. In Greek, *to* (the *o* is short, as in 'tock') is the neuter form of the definite article – the word for 'the'. In ordinary usage *apeiron* referred to unenclosed or indeterminate areas, much as we might look at open moorland or desert and think of it as 'boundless'. Anaximander gives the word a special meaning: 'the unlimited', or 'the infinite' – something spatially infinite, everlasting, indeterminate, out of which all known things emerge and into which they will be resolved 'in accordance with the arrangement made by time'. The words in quotation marks are recorded by Simplicus and are the first known utterance of European science. They are Anaximander's attempt to form the concept that we easily refer to as 'the laws of nature' – laws which at that time were unformulated, and for which no general term like 'laws of nature' existed.

So if the earth was formed from *to apeiron*, how did this happen? Anaximander has an answer that also disposes of Thales' problem about what the earth rests on: it rests on nothing. The earth is formed by a vortex in *to apeiron*. Stir a pot of liquid with bits in it, and the bits will tend to congregate in the middle of the vortex. And so the earth was formed – not flat and floating on water like a lid, but as a cylinder, supported by nothing, because in the infinite, as Aristotle explains on behalf of Anaximander, there is 'indifference': 'that which is situated at the centre and is equally related to the extremities has no impulse to move in one direction rather than any other … hence it remains at rest' (*On the Heavens*, II). The ancient problem about the immobility of the earth arose from two apparently contrary observations: the first that the earth is still, not falling; and the second, that everything falls unless it is supported by something. Anaximander's (or Aristotle's) appeal to 'indifference' is about as far as can be reached until the beginning of a conception of gravity or attraction after 300 BC.

But if the earth was formed from *to apeiron*, how is it that life, particularly the frail and vulnerable beginnings of life that are babies, took hold? Anaximander appears to have had two parts to his answer. The first is this: the land was formed by the drying-out of what he took to be the primeval mud – a process he could see, as the Meander silted up the seashore near Miletus. The occurrence of what we call fossils, which Anaximander seems to have regarded as the dried impressions of things set in the mud, provided some evidence. In the second part of his attempt to explain life's origins, Anaximander supposes that the first animals came into being in the mud, encased in prickly barks, and (as Aetius reports, in the late 1st century AD) 'as they reached maturity they moved out on to the drier parts where their barks split and they survived in a different form for a brief while'. This is not Darwinian evolution, nor is it Aristotle's mistaken doctrine of the immutability of species, but it is some sort of answer to the question of how life began. It is wrong, but it is thought-provoking.

The Milesians' questions were new and so, for all its long-ago strangeness, was the manner of their answering. It marks the beginning of what might be called 'scientific method': answers founded on some sort of reasoning and evidence, subject to correction or to alternative theories propounded by others, and, above all, not enshrined in dogmatic systems affirmed as ultimate religious truth. In that sense Thales, Anaximander and Anaximenes set human enquiry on a course from which it has only diverged at peril: the course of free enquiry, which Socrates was to describe definitively as 'following where the evidence leads'.

Why Miletus?

Why did these attempts to understand the universe begin at Miletus and not, say, at Babylon, where the movements of the heavenly bodies –

sun, moon and stars (including the planets, 'the wanderers') – had long been mapped in mathematical detail, and where algebraic mathematics was remarkably advanced?

We cannot know, but the apparent reason is that the mapping, and hence prediction, of the movement of the heavenly bodies was undertaken at Babylon and elsewhere for religious and astrological ends – to fix the dates of festivals, seed time and harvest – and for predicting political events. The data was, moreover, collected by priests, whose purposes were not served by asking questions about the nature of what was observed. The stars are the gods', or God's, handiwork, and that is all you need to know – or perhaps should know. So what makes Miletus in particular, and Ionia in general, different?

In the 6th century BC Miletus was an independent, powerful and successful trading city, having commerce with Syria and Egypt by sea, and probably with Persia and Mesopotamia by land. Its merchants and leading citizens would thus have had the opportunity to encounter the astronomical data amassed in Mesopotamia, as well as the practical geometry of Egypt. In short, they had access to important sources of information.

Second, Miletus was rich enough ('the chief ornament of Ionia', as Herodotus remarks) and powerful enough to have men with the leisure to think and argue without worrying over much about where the next meal was coming from or how to deal with the next enemy. Moreover, the right sort of people were there – people with open minds free to speculate and argue with others without fear of private hates or civic commotion.

Finally, but crucially, Miletus was a city in which religion – as in the Ionian world in general, and for long in the Hellenic world that followed it – was a civic activity in which the leading citizens undertook almost all religious duties, not out of commitment but *de facto*. The religion itself consisted of observances, ceremonies, festivals, offerings, the reading of signs that indicated the favour or opposition of the gods to some proposed course of action, respect for the gods and their sacred places, and numerous minor superstitions. As is clear from Homer and Hesiod, the gods are a part of this world, not another order of being. There is no 'spirit world' from which the physical world was created. It may be difficult for some of us to grasp the idea, but the distinction between 'spiritual' and 'material', between this world and another different in kind, scarcely existed in Ionia in the 6th century BC. There was one world, some of whose inhabitants were immortal, exceptionally powerful and usually invisible. They were the gods. No offence could be caused to them by investigating the nature of the eternal universe that both we and they shared. There are strong suggestions of an early two-world belief in Xenophanes, and they are stronger still in the cult Pythagoras founded in the west, but it is not until Plato that the two-world metaphysic of reality received a full, rational and systematic statement – one that has ever since had a profound influence upon all Western beliefs.

The way leads on: Presocratic philosophy
What happens next is diffuse and confusing. The term 'Presocratic philosophy' covers a vague range of dates and contains so many names, conflicting ideas and ill-recorded arguments that it is impossible to give a brief account. In practice, it includes more or less any thinker (excluding Plato) who was born or flourished before the death of Socrates in 399 BC.

There are three or four well-known names, about thirty that might be recognized, and an expert could list another fifty or so. They include the Ionian originals Pythagoras, Xenophanes and Heraclitus, whose lives overlapped with those of the Milesians. There was an important group who moved to or lived in southern Italy or Sicily – the Eleatics – who provoked the first philosophical, as opposed to physical, questions. Others, mostly a little later, lived on the coast of the north Aegean and returned to physicalist speculations. Finally, there was a large number of itinerant teachers of lifemanship, or how to get on in society: the Sophists, the last and greatest of whom was Socrates.

Of these selected groups, the Ionian originals and the Eleatics are the subject of the following chapter. The physicalists, mainly Leucippus and Democritus, form a natural introduction to Epicurus and the atomic theory in Chapter 7. The Sophists are touched upon in Chapter 5 as a preliminary to Plato.

4

Ionia and Western Greece: Laws, Numbers and Reality

For anyone who has the enterprise or good luck to visit Italy south of Naples, it is easy to see the ruins of the Classical ages of Greece and Rome. It is much more difficult to grasp the fact that, for their first six hundred years or so, the quintessentially Italian towns in the area were entirely Greek.

The area known to the Romans as *Magna Graecia* and to the Greeks as *Megale Hellas* was variously defined at different periods, but it always included the cities from Cyme (usually known by its Latin name Cumae), 16 km (10 miles) north-west of Naples, to those on the toe and heel of Italy. Sometimes Sicily was included under the heading. The Hellenic cities were founded in the 8th to 6th centuries BC as colonies from mainland Greece – remarkably early settlements established for trade or to receive overflow populations from their mother city. Cumae, one of the earliest colonies, was established in about 740 BC, Croton in *c.* 710 BC, Paestum (founded as Poseidonia) in *c.* 600 BC, and Elea, 60 km (37 miles) south of Paestum, in *c.* 540 BC.

In the history of ideas, Croton (modern Crotone) and Elea (modern Castellamare) are in their own ways almost as significant as Miletus. It was to the infant city of Croton that Pythagoras emigrated from Samos, and there founded the semi-religious cult that bears his name, as well as developing arithmetical geometry and the mathematical analysis of music. Xenophanes resided in the city for a long period. Parmenides was born in Elea, and together with Zeno established a distinctive 'school' of philosophy there (a set of related ideas taught to and discussed with other men), which for the first time explicitly raised questions beyond those asked by the Milesian physicalists, such as: What is real? What is motion? Can what is real be subjected to unlimited real division? How does our language relate to what is real?

These are the first philosophical or metaphysical ('behind nature') questions. They still trouble us. Their seeds can perhaps be traced to the Ionian originals Xenophanes and Pythagoras; but the third man I included in that odd category – Heraclitus – is so strange and so influential that I shall make room for him below, after the Pythagoreans and before the Eleatics.

The Pythagoreans

The theorem attributed to Pythagoras concerning the square on the hypotenuse has given his name a familiarity denied to the man himself. He and his cult were both revered and derided in antiquity, but even then little was known for certain about Pythagoras as an individual.

Pythagoras was a native of the island of Samos, where he was born in about 570 BC. Heraclitus, about thirty years his junior, is scathing (as he is about most people, so perhaps we shouldn't take too much notice): 'Pythagoras … practised research most of all men, and making extracts from these writings claimed as his own a wisdom that was only much learning.' And again: 'Much learning does not teach understanding, or Hesiod and Pythagoras would have been taught it.'

With or without understanding, the book-learned Pythagoras seems to have remained on Samos until about 530, when, disaffected with the ruling elite, he left for the newly founded colony of Croton. There, according to Diogenes Laertius in *c.* AD 210,

> He and his followers were held in great esteem; for being
> nearly three hundred in number, so well did they govern
> the state that its constitution was in effect a true aristocracy –
> government by the best.

Diogenes follows this gem of information with about twenty pages of gossip – 'So and so says that he … Others say …' – from which, in conjunction with other reports, we may conclude that Pythagoras established a sect or school in Croton from which two related traditions emerge: the mathematical and the mystical.

Concerning the mathematical, Aristotle, in Book I of the *Metaphysics*, writing relatively near to Pythagoras' life – say about 170 years after his death – is curt to the point of censure:

> The so-called Pythagoreans applied themselves to mathematics
> … and through studying it they came to believe that its
> principles are the principles of everything … Whatever
> analogues to the processes and parts of the heavens and to
> the whole order of the universe they could exhibit in numbers
> and proportions, these they collected and correlated; and if
> there was any deficiency anywhere, they made haste to supply
> it, in order to make their system a connected whole.

Even without the lengthy analysis required to unpack in full Aristotle's criticisms of Pythagoras, it will be clear that at best he regards him as careless, and at worst as a charlatan.

The over-grand conclusion that number proportions were the principles that underlay everything probably derived from one remarkable discovery attributed to Pythagoras – that the basic melodic framework of the octave on the seven-stringed Greek lyre could be expressed as a simple numerical ratio between the first four integers: the musical scale. The discovery became confused with number mysticism, but it also lit the fuse that eventually led to the explosion of knowledge in the application of mathematical descriptions to physics.

On the other hand, Pythagoras' theorem did not originate with him. As part of a system of arithmetical geometry it may well be his, but its practical application in building – especially in the case of the 3:4:5 right-angle triangle – had been known to Egyptian land-surveyors for centuries.

The mystic cult of the Pythagoreans – partly associated with number magic, 'the music of the spheres', perfect proportions, and so on – has features that enthralled and amused the ancients as much as they do us. Their big philosophical (or religious, depending on the point of view) thesis was the separation of body and soul in a way scarcely hinted at in the Homeric naturalism of living human animal and waning post-mortem wraith. The Pythagoreans believed in the transmigration, or 'metempsychosis', of souls from one living thing to another at death. They reasoned that the soul, or the continuing identity of the person, has a previous existence in a succession of living things, and will be reincarnated in future living things, not necessarily all of them men or women. The doctrine has interesting and at times ludicrous consequences that were even seized upon by Xenophanes, an exact contemporary of Pythagoras, who tells this story about him:

> On one occasion he was passing by when a man was beating
> a dog, and they say he took pity on the animal and said,
> 'Stop it! It is the soul of a friend of mine. I recognized him
> when I heard its voice.'

Hundreds of years later the delightful satirist Lucian lampooned the Pythagoreans mercilessly in several of his dialogues. For example, in *The Dream* an articulate cock, the current embodiment of Pythagoras, is asked why he made a law against eating meat or beans. On being pressed for an answer, he says in a show of embarrassment:

> It was nothing sensible or wise, but I perceived that if I made
> laws that were ordinary and just like those of run-of-the-mill
> legislators, I should not induce men to wonder at me, whereas
> the more I departed from the normal, the more of a figure
> I should cut, I thought, in men's eyes. Therefore I chose
> outlandish rules, keeping the reason for them secret so that
> one man might guess one thing and one another. Look here,
> you're laughing at me!

'Not at you, but at your followers,' comes the answer. In another dialogue, *Philosophies for Sale*, Lucian puts it all in one sentence. In answer to the question, 'What does Pythagoras know best?' he says: 'Arithmetic, astronomy, charlatanry, geometry, music and quackery.' Conjecture surrounding the possible reason for prohibiting the eating of meat centred upon fears that you might, for instance, be munching on the reincarnation of your grandmother. Those concerning the injunction against beans varied between the frivolous and the obscene.

Xenophanes of Colophon
Xenophanes was an elegiac poet of considerable distinction, who also expressed interesting quasi-philosophical thoughts. Aristotle dismisses him as simplistic and primitive. He was born in Colophon, in

Ionia, in about 570 BC, and departed from his native city when he was 25 years old, probably to escape the newly established Persian suzerainty. For the rest of his long life (he lived to be at least 92), he was a wanderer in Magna Graecia and a long-term resident in several Sicilian cities – as well, very probably, as Elea and Croton. Two seminal ideas originate with him.

The most important is his conception of a single god that has no anthropomorphic qualities, bodily or mental, and in particular none of the 'shameful' characteristics Hesiod and Homer attributed to the gods. In one of the fragmentary quotations that survive, he observes: 'If oxen and horses and lions had hands or could draw with hands … horses would draw pictures of gods like horses, and oxen of gods like oxen'; but 'There is one god, among gods and men the greatest [NB: this 'one god' is not alone among gods], not at all like mortals in body or in mind.' This one god 'sees as a whole, thinks as a whole, and hears as a whole'. But 'without toil he sets everything in motion by the thought of his mind', and 'he always remains in the same place, not moving at all.' These hints were to be taken up by Parmenides.

This talk about an absolutely non-human god is the beginning of Greek philosophical monotheism, of Aristotle's 'unmoved mover'. But, as with Aristotle's god, the thing is too remote and dehumanized to be identified with the Jewish god, or to anticipate the Christian or Islamic conceptions of deity, which have at least some mental features like our own so that we can speak of them as loving, just, forgiving, etc.

The second seminal idea we find in Xenophanes' surviving thoughts is the beginning of scepticism with regard to the senses, with the implication that there is a gap between what seems to us and what is real: 'All are appearances that exist for mortals to look at'; and again: 'Let these things be stated as conjectural only, similar to reality.' And most explicitly:

> And as for certain truth, no man has seen it, nor will there
> ever be a man who knows about the gods and about all the
> things I mention. For if he succeeds to the full in saying
> what is completely true, he himself is nevertheless unaware
> of it, and opinion covers all things.

Pythagoras, reborn as a cockerel, attempts to draw a right-angle.

As with modern parking regulations, so with difficult or fragmentary ancient texts – the authorities disagree. But it is beyond dispute that, in Hellenistic philosophy after Aristotle, scepticism about the way language relates to reality, and more radically about how sense experience that is necessarily in us relates to what is real outside us, was rampant. In fact, the questions that such philosophical scepticism raises have never gone away, and Xenophanes helped to start them. Moreover, because of the period in which he was commenting, Xenophanes would have been familiar with the conflicting theories of Heraclitus of Ephesus (that everything is in a state of change) and of Parmenides of Elea (that reality is one and motionless) – opposing views that invite scepticism about the possibility of truth, or of knowing that you have it even when you do indeed have it. This is a change from Homer. In the *Iliad*, there is only a sad acceptance of our lack of knowledge: 'You are goddesses and are present and know all things, but we hear only a rumour and know nothing' (II.484–86). For Xenophanes and those who followed, such doubts are a rational response to thought philosophical questions.

Heraclitus of Ephesus
Heraclitus 'the Dark', as he was sometimes called, is the third of the highly individualistic group I have named the 'Ionian originals'. He was born in Ephesus in about 540 BC, and died there at about the age of 60. From 546 onwards Ephesus was part of the Persian Empire, so Heraclitus, intellectually the most autocratic of men, was throughout his life a subject of the Persian king.

It may well be that he wrote no continuously argued book, but enough of his carefully crafted, enigmatic sayings and challenging observations survive in disconnected sound bites to fill about ten modern printed pages. Among the Presocratics a larger number of fragments survive only from Democritus, but he was a prolific writer. Heraclitus was not. He is very quotable:

Magnanimity consists in enduring tactlessness with mildness.

The foolish learn sense through misfortune.

An enemy is not he who injures, but he who wishes to do so.

Not all relations are friends: only those who agree with
us about what is useful.

Good things come with difficulty if one seeks; bad things
come without the asking.

Much has been written about this impressive man, and the crafted
intensity of so many of his utterances will always give rise to argument. The following brief summary may give some idea of his main
themes without provoking too many academics into murderous denunciations of the present writer.

The sentences that probably commenced his book, if indeed he
wrote one, are these:

(Thus says Heraclitus of Ephesus.) And of this account [*logos*]
which is the case always men prove to have no understanding,
both before they hear it and when first they have heard it. All
things happen in accordance with this *logos*, but men seem like
untried novices when they make trial of such words and facts
as I recount by dividing up each thing according to its nature
[*phusis*] and saying how it is.

The ambiguities ('always', for instance, could relate to 'which is the case'
or to 'men') are deliberate and typical of Heraclitus, not merely bad
translations. The word *logos* has many meanings in Classical philosophy,
and they vary over time and according the intentions of the writer.
Heraclitus was writing early in the history of philosophy; and his *logos*
is close to the basic meaning of 'story' or 'account', but with the larger
sense of an account that explains the nature of a thing, or a law to
explain the way all things work. What can we say about such an account,
given that either he never stated it in full or the statement is lost?

We can say that the law is objective. It relates to things external
to us, but includes us in its scope. It can be reached through observation of the world: 'All that can be learnt about by seeing and hearing,
this I value highest.' It has something to do with the conflict of opposites. In a trivial, linguistic sense, 'up' and 'down' are opposites, but
the words are only understandable in relation to each other; this

applies also to 'hot' and 'cold', 'moist' and 'dry', and other qualities with contrasting extremes. In nature, Heraclitus seems to be saying, there is something similar: an ever changing contrast and conflict between fire, and objects that have stability in some features for some time. Heraclitus uses the words 'kindles' and 'quenches'. Everything is altering according to an understandable true account, and in a process that should be called 'strife'. In this strife, the intelligible source of change is fire; in human affairs it is war. (Lenin much approved of Heraclitus!)

From this prickly heap of thoughts, Heraclitus' most celebrated utterance can be seen to follow. Since the law of nature, *logos,* is the continuous, dynamic opposition between fire and things, no thing has absolute permanence. What is real is ever changing: 'It is not possible to step into the same river twice.' This is obviously true in the sense that some things that we call by an enduring name and regard as the same over time – the river Thames, for example – are constantly altering. But Heraclitus is saying something much wider and less obvious than this. He is saying, via the striking example of the river, something about the nature of reality that can be established by observation: that everything is always changing in *some* respects. And that is the open challenge the natural sciences are still taking up – to give content to Heraclitus' *logos.*

One last comment: The word for 'god' occurs in a number of Heraclitus' sayings, and much learned ink has been spilled over the subject. But whatever 'god' is for him, it is not the God modern men and women might envisage. Heraclitus' god is more like the underlying unity and coherence of the universe, perhaps justifying the description intelligent, but certainly not partial to humanity: 'To god all things are beautiful, good and just'; 'God is day–night, summer–winter, war–peace, satiety–famine'. God is the ordered structure of all that is – an idea to bear splendid development with the Stoics, who revered Heraclitus and who spoke of god as ever-living fire – the reason of all order in nature.

The Eleatics

Parmenides (*c.* 510–after 450) and Zeno, his junior by about twenty-five years, both citizens of Elea, were the first to propound philosophical arguments in a full modern sense, if not in a full modern form. In the case of Parmenides, disentangling the astoundingly complex argument contained in the large fragments of his philosophical poem (yes, poem) that survive can still frighten the lecturer without informing the student. In the case of Zeno, whose paradoxes about infinite divisibility are reported in Aristotle's *Physics,* the case is different. Although the problems he raised are still among the profoundest and most intractable in mathematics and philosophy, seeing what they are is not all that difficult.

I shall not try to anaesthetize you with a discussion of Parmenides' argument. One long sentence from its beginning will give its flavour:

> The ways of enquiry which alone are to be thought: the one
> that IT IS, and it is not possible for IT NOT TO BE, is the way
> of credibility, for it follows truth; the other, that IT IS NOT, and
> that it is bound NOT TO BE: this I tell you is a path that cannot
> be explored; for you could neither recognize that which IS
> NOT, nor express it ... That which is possible to think is
> identical with that which can BE ... BEING has no coming-into-
> being ... it is a whole, without motion and without end ...
> It IS now, a whole all together, ONE, continuous ...

Very well, on first (and subsequent?) reading this is gobbledygook. The preliminary sorting out must consist of separating three uses of the verb 'to be', not distinguished until after Parmenides and muddled – to some effect – by him.

They are the *is* of existence – 'There is (exists) water on the moon'; the *is* of predication – 'The moon is (has the characteristic) cold' and the *is* of identity – 'The Morning Star *is* (the same as) the Evening Star'. But there is more here than just a confusion. Parmenides is asserting that the language division 'exists/does not exist' is also the division between what can intelligibly be said and what cannot be said; and, in turn, that distinction is also the distinction between what exists and is real, and what does not exist and is not real. Furthermore, what exists and is real, is what it is and nothing else. So what is real is one and motionless.

If you feel confused, you are probably feeling much as Diogenes Laertius did in about AD 210. He is often remarkably forthcoming about the remotest figures, but concerning Parmenides he obviously hasn't a clue. After a few paragraphs of silly anecdotes that have nothing to do with philosophy, he abandons the matter. If you want to be different, look at the further reading at the end of this chapter.

The paradoxes of Zeno of Elea

According to Parmenides' argument – and when all is said, it is an argument, not the assertion of some sort of metaphysical mysticism – reality is single and unchanging, i.e. it is motionless. Zeno's paradoxes of motion are designed to show that to suppose otherwise – that motion is real – is to show up 'still greater absurdities'.

Aristotle records the four paradoxes in Book IV of the *Physics*. Our immediate response to them will probably be the same as Aristotle's, but without the brilliant clarity of his, on this occasion not quite conclusive, reasoning. He and we will say that the paradoxes are obviously in some way misleading in view of what we all see and know happens. But beware of over-hasty dismissal, lest you fall foul of the rebuke of one of the 20th century's greatest mathematical philosophers, Bertrand Russell: 'Having invented four arguments, all immeasurably subtle and profound, the grossness of subsequent philosophers pronounced him to be a mere ingenious juggler, and his arguments to be one and all sophisms.' I'll omit the fourth paradox, which is cumbersome to describe or discuss.

1 **The Dichotomy or The Race Course.** In this paradox Zeno declares that movement is impossible because, however near a moving object (e.g. a runner) is to any point (e.g. the finishing line), it (or he or she) will always have to cover half the distance first, and, before that, half of that first distance, and so on, halving the first distance to be traversed without end. The moving object, therefore, can never get started. In diagrammatic form, the paradox looks like this:

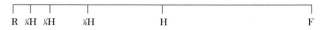

In order for R to get to F, it must first get to H, halfway. But in order to get to H, it must first get to ½H. But in order to get to

½H, it must first get to half of ½H (i.e. ¼H). In order to get to ¼H, it must get to ⅛H, and before that to ⅟₁₆H, and before that to ⅟₃₂H, and before that to ⅟₆₄H, and so on without end. So the runner does not start.

2 **Achilles and the Tortoise.** Aristotle himself says, 'The second is what is known as the "Achilles". It purports to show that the slowest will never be overtaken by the swiftest, inasmuch as, reckoning from any given moment, the pursuer, before he can reach the pursued, must reach the point from which the pursued started at that moment. And so the slower will always be some distance in front of the swifter.'

The arithmetic of the argument works for any lead given by Achilles to the tortoise at the start, but it can be seen most simply by supposing that Achilles (apparently by far the swifter) agrees to give the tortoise (apparently by far the slower) half the course as a generous start. So the situation is this:

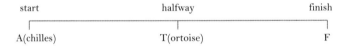

start   halfway   finish

A(chilles)   T(ortoise)   F

Let us now suppose, to make the presentation realistic, that we have an exceptionally athletic tortoise, and that whatever speed Achilles runs at, Tortoise at least manages to get going and cover some distance rather than just sitting still and contemplating the universe between its feet, in the way tortoises do. By the time A has got to where T started (call it T_1), Tortoise has reached T_2 (some distance), thus:

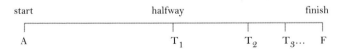

start   halfway   finish

A T_1 T_2 T_3...   F

By the time A has got to T_2, Tortoise has got a little farther, say to T_3. By the time A has got to T_3, T has run a little farther, and so on for ever. At each time interval, A will always have got to where T was, but T will have got a little farther, however small that bit farther is reckoned to be. So A never catches T.

Another version of the Achilles paradox makes it clear that the logical/mathematical problem it poses is the obverse of the Dichotomy. Trundle the Tortoise off the racetrack and simply give Achilles the task of getting from the start to the finish. In order to get to F, he must get halfway. In order to get from halfway to F, he must traverse half of the distance that remains. Having got here, he must traverse half of the remaining distance, and so on ad infinitum, halving the distance yet to be traversed without ever reaching F.

In short, the Dichotomy shows that the runner cannot start; the Achilles that he cannot finish. So motion is an illusion, or our description of it is wrong.

3 The Arrow. This paradox argues that in the present 'now', a body in motion, such as an arrow, occupies a place of its own size and is therefore at rest: it is where it is. But since it is in a 'now' throughout its apparent movement, and therefore occupies a place of its own size at every 'now', in reality it is always at rest.

I remember at school when our music master, apparently despairing of our aesthetic sensibilities, recounted the Arrow paradox. Our form wag, M. E . Clarke, volunteered: 'Sir, you run on ahead, and I'll fire the arrow.' Aristotle was equally brisk: 'It rests on the assumption that time is made up of *nows*, and if this be not granted, the paradox fails.' He is similarly short with the Achilles: 'The thing that is ahead is not overtaken while it is ahead, but none the less it is overtaken if Zeno will allow it to traverse to the end of its finite distance.' And mathematicians making assumptions about convergent series, as well as the Clarkes and Aristotles of this world, will all agree that the paradoxes do not represent what happens (what seems to happen, Zeno would say). The problem remains that, under the descriptions given, Achilles cannot start and cannot finish, let alone reach the end of the racecourse, as Aristotle wishes to allow. With the Arrow, the question is precisely whether time is made up of a series of 'nows'; and, if not, what is time? The problem

Zeno running away from an arrow in flight.

lies not in what we all know happens, but in the description of what happens (Zeno-speak: 'appears to happen'). This description has the disconcerting implication that Parmenides is right – in reality, nothing can move.

Before you solve the paradoxes for yourself, consider this final point, using the version of the Achilles in which the runner cannot reach the finish. The core of the paradox can be stated thus: *either* the tiny distance that always seems to remain between the runner and the finish is a real distance, *or* it is not a real distance.

If it is a real distance, then it really can be halved, and the runner's problem about reaching the finish continues. If it is not a real distance, you have a choice of two alternatives. Why is it not a real distance when the tiny distance before it was real and could be halved? Second, if at some point in halving real distances we reach something that is not a real distance, how is it that the real distance can apparently be made up of the sum of all the unreal distances? In any case, all this is better than Sudoku, is it not?

* * *

Read on. The Presocratics are numerous and widely dispersed. More will be said about some of them later, but much will be omitted. A lucid and simple survey is in J. V. Luce's *An Introduction to Greek Philosophy* (London, 1992). Bertrand Russell's *History of Western Philosophy* (London, 1945; revd edn 2009) is cogent and exciting concerning the Presocratics. A hardworking study is E. Hussey's *The Presocratics* (London, 1972). The most exhaustive, and at times exhausting, study is J. Barnes's *The Presocratic Philosophers* (London, 1982; revd edn 1999). All these works include the Milesian physicalists among the Presocratics.

There is no standard way of referring to the surviving fragments of the Presocratics. They have been assembled in English translations by several authorities, including Kathleen Freeman, *Ancilla to the Pre-Socratic Philosophers* (Oxford, 1947), Jonathan Barnes, *Early Greek Philosophy* (Harmondsworth, 1987) and Robin Waterfield, *The First Philosophers* (Oxford, 2000).

5

Athens: Socrates,
Plato and Other Worlds

The years of Athens' greatest political power and towering cultural achievements lay mostly between the battle of Plataea in 479 BC, when the Persian threat to the Greek mainland was removed, and the fall of Athens to Sparta in 404, at the end of the protracted Peloponnesian Wars that had begun in 431. This is the age of Pericles, which witnessed the building of the Parthenon, the plays of Sophocles, Euripides and Aristophanes, and, towards its end, the beginnings of philosophy in Athens in the persons of Anaxagoras, Protagoras, and the travelling teachers known as Sophists, culminating with the suburban Athenian Socrates (469–399 BC). However, the real and recorded triumph of the Athenian philosophers, and the establishment of Athens as the primary centre of philosophical teaching for about one thousand years, came after the defeat of 404.

Plato (427–347 BC) was a young Athenian aristocrat at the time of the city's defeat, and he happened to be ill during the trial and execution of Socrates in 399. All his vast philosophical writings date from after that time, when Athens was slowly and painfully recovering.

Aristotle, greatest of all philosophers, was not even born until 384, and not in Athens, to which he came in order to be taught by Plato. He returned there to teach in his own right between 335 and 323, while his erstwhile pupil, Alexander the Great, was destroying the Persian Empire – that long-persisting affront to everything Hellenic.

Socrates: Sophists and methods
For all their enigmatic difficulty, the arguments of Parmenides and Zeno spread widely in the Hellenic world during the half-century between 450 and 400. In conjunction with the political freedom and stability of Athens, they provoked responses among both the Sophists

and those physicalists – notably Democritus in far-off Abdera – who were still developing the ideas that had begun in Miletus. These responses represented the beginning of scepticism, humanism, mysticism and atomism.

The sceptical reaction was typified by Protagoras of Abdera, who maintained that we cannot refute Parmenides' arguments. We cannot distinguish between one physicalist conjecture about the nature of things and another by argument, partly because we do not have clear evidence one way or the other, and partly because if we had, we would not know that we had it; and anyway it would all be undermined by Parmenides or Zeno. So then comes the enduring common-sense reply to excessive despair about knowing anything properly: we must rely upon our senses. There is no alternative, and we may as well ignore the metaphysical horrors of the sort Parmenides was the first to uncover, and get on with living in the best way we can.

Eleatic metaphysics thus provoked a scepticism regarding philosophical conclusions and certain knowledge, and also a concern with human arrangements – politics, ethics and how to get on in civil society. This was the trade of paid itinerant wisdom-mongers, the Sophists. We might call it the 'teaching of lifemanship'.

It seems that the moral and ethical dimensions of life were in no way the concern of the earliest Milesian physicalists. They were the first scientists, speculating about the nature of the universe, not about human weal and woe. After the Sophists, such disinterested physicalism never again appeared among those who claimed to be philosophers. Even the greatest of the Presocratic physicalists, Democritus, developed the atomic theory in parallel with ethical advice and aphorisms that add up to a vaguely utilitarian account of human society. Aristotle is a scientist, a metaphysician *and* a moral philosopher. After Aristotle, the Epicureans and the Stoics each had sophisticated accounts of the natural universe, but they had them in company with a way of life which they argued was in harmony with the physical universe, and a realistic way of coping with our place in it.

The Sophists' employers were those who wanted to prosper and to achieve political importance in the sort of democratic *polis* Athens had come to exemplify. In practice, that meant influencing a large assembly through public speaking. Thus the Sophists were above all teachers of oratory and of what went with it: rhetoric, the refutation of opposing arguments (which so often led to a confusion between the power of the spoken word and valid reasoning), a focus upon the subject under debate, and eventually language, grammar and logic. They were also questioners of established religions and observances, and of social and political conventions – a safe undertaking in the Athens of Pericles, but much more precarious in the darker and increasingly desperate Athens of the Peloponnesian Wars and after.

All wars, even our own ideological wars against racism, sexism and the rest, close down certain freedoms of speech. In Athens, the greatest casualty of the closedown was Socrates. By some he was regarded as a nuisance, a 'gadfly', but his deep questioning went far beyond that of any of his predecessors or contemporaries.

Socrates wrote nothing. He is, however, conspicuous in the writings of others. He appears in Aristophanes' play *The Clouds* (423 BC), lampooned as the purveyor of absurdly over-clever arguments. (Nonetheless, Plato's *Symposium* portrays Socrates and Aristophanes as being on good terms at a dinner party.) He features in the *Memorabilia* of Xenophon, the writer and soldier, and also in his *Symposium* and *Apology* – the last a version of Socrates' defence at his trial. Socrates is portrayed as the main speaker in almost all of Plato's early dialogues and in most of his middle-period writings. His late works – conspicuously his longest and last work, the *Laws* – scarcely mention Socrates.

Plato makes it difficult to distinguish the real Socrates from the Socrates who is used as a voice to express Plato's own arguments. But we can distinguish in Plato, and less clearly in Xenophon, a technique of philosophical enquiry that became known as the 'Socratic method'. It has been used ever since.

The method is the conversational, non-aggressive questioning of the assumptions we make about what we know or what something is. Get someone to assert a definition of something such as love, justice, knowledge, fairness, piety or beauty. The discussion may begin with a self-serving definition: 'Justice is what I am dealing out now', or 'Fairness is what we have enacted in all our legislation'. Or it may begin with a genuine attempt at true definition: 'Knowledge is perception'. The end of the process is not certainty, but a clearer understanding of what the problems are, and a realization that those things we may unthinkingly take as obvious in life or society or language are seldom as obvious as we first suppose. In Plato's *Theaetetus*, Socrates famously compares himself to a midwife: he does not produce truths himself, but 'The triumph of my art is in thoroughly examining whether the thought which the mind of the young man brings forth is false and life-less, or fertile and true.' This is the critical art that, in the dark days of Athens' defeat, led to Socrates' arraignment on charges trumped up by leaders under Spartan influence who found him an irritation. As a result of his politically inconvenient integrity, he was executed, but with his own assent as a loyal member of the state.

Socrates: The ideal of integrity

Plato wrote four dialogues about the last days of Socrates. The *Euthyphro* takes place when Socrates is awaiting trial on the charge of impiety. It asks what 'piety' (dutiful respect, or giving each his due – not quite the modern meaning of the English word) is. In the course of the discussion, it raises one of religion's and morality's most funda-mental questions: is goodness that which all the gods love (i.e. do the gods, or does God, define what is good?), or do all the gods, or does God, love what is good? (i.e. do the gods endorse what is, independ-ently of them, good?). The drift of argument favours the second alternative, but, with the definition of piety unresolved, the main char-acter, Euthyphro, departs in a hurry, leaving Socrates to face a charge of contravening something undefined. In the *Apology* we are offered an account of Socrates' defence at his trial. Almost certainly his accusers wanted him out of the way, not dead. Socrates merely ridiculed the charge, and when he was found guilty by 280 to 220 – Athenian juries were large! – he suggested that, as a benefactor to the city, he ought to be rewarded. In the last sentence of the dialogue, Socrates concludes: 'The hour of departure has come, and we go our ways – I to die, and you to live. Which is better only god knows.'

In the *Crito* Socrates is awaiting the time of execution. Crito, an old friend, brings a plan of escape. (It is quite likely that the authorities wanted him to escape, to avoid possible later contumely for having killed him.) But Socrates will not oblige. There is an implicit agree-ment, he contends, with the state that has nurtured and preserved you, to abide by its laws and judgments even if, at the end, they harm you. The important thing is not only to have life, but to live honourably.

It is probable that the *Euthyphro, Apology* and *Crito* were written soon after Socrates' death. In particular the *Apology* looks historically accurate. Many people were present at the trial, and at least some of them would have read or heard Plato's account and would have objected had it been a falsification. But the dialogue dealing with Socrates' execution, the *Phaedo*, was written perhaps twenty or thirty years after the event. In that sense it has a similar relationship to the death of Socrates as the earliest gospels have to the death of Jesus. Plato was not himself an eyewitness, but he knew eyewitnesses who at the time would have told him about Socrates' death.

Aside from the narrative account of the execution (by poisoned wine, voluntarily taken), the dialogue is a powerful presentation of the this world/other world dichotomy, the other world consisting of ideal forms (to be explained later) – the world of perfect knowledge of the good to which Socrates expects to be going. His last recorded words are, somewhat oddly one might think, 'Crito, I owe a cock to Asclepius; will you remember to pay my debt?' He is observing piety to the god. As an honourable man, he is fulfilling an obligation that will soon be incurred: Asclepius, the god of healing, is about to cure him of the ills of life.

Socrates' thoughts about death, and his expectations, are made abundantly clear in the *Phaedo*, but his conclusion in the *Apology* is the same and worth quoting at length. There are two alternatives:

Either death is a state of nothingness and utter
unconsciousness, or, as some men say, there is a change and a
migration of the soul from this world to another. Now if you
suppose that there is no consciousness, but a sleep like the
sleep of him who is undisturbed ever by dreams, death will be
an unspeakable gain. For if a person were to select the night
in which his sleep was undisturbed even by dreams, and were
to compare with this the other days and nights of his life, and
were then to tell us how many days and nights he had passed
better and more pleasantly than this one ... I think no man
will find many ... Now if death be of such a nature, I say
that to die is gain; for eternity is then only a single night.

> But if death is the journey to another place … what good,
> oh my friends and judges, can be greater than this?

In the *Crito*, the good is meeting the wise and excellent. In the *Phaedo*, it is encountering the ultimate realities that lie beyond the shadowy knowledge and imperfections of this world.

Socrates is philosophy's first and most renowned sacrifice to the integrity of a person and to the rightness of allowing reason to lead where it will. None better has ever been provided.

Plato

The Presocratics are known to us only through the survival of fragmentary quotations in the works of later authors. Socrates is well known to us but only through the writings of his contemporaries. Suddenly with Plato we have everything. Uniquely among ancient philosophers, we have all that he wrote – and a bit more, in the form of doubtful works attributed to him. The result is a body of writings that defies summary and takes a lifetime to master. I will pick out just two related topics that figure large. They are the question 'What is knowledge?', and one of its answers: that knowledge relates to ideal forms that exist as realities in another world accessible to the intellect, but perhaps only to be encountered in full after the soul (or intellectual soul) is freed from the body by death.

What is knowledge?

Plato gives two answers. There is the answer expressed in terms of the 'theory of forms'. This dominates the *Republic*, the *Phaedo*, and other dialogues written within twenty years or so of Socrates' death in 399 BC. Let us call this the 'two-world answer'. The second is in the *Theaetetus*, which was written after 369. The *Theaetetus* is the first ever work on the subject we now call epistemology – the theory of knowledge – and it is still one of the best. It makes no mention of the two-world answer. Whether this is because Plato had given it up (Aristotle – his pupil – demolished it in his *Metaphysics*) or because he was providing a parallel linguistic account is hotly debated but undecidable. I'll call the *Theaetetus* account the 'analytic answer'.

1 **The analytic answer.** The analytic answer is ultimately not a complete answer, but rather the examination and rejection of a number of ever better suggestions that result – in a typically Socratic way – in a clearer understanding of the issues. The outline, omitting all Plato's wonderfully ingenious metaphors, examples and arguments, consists in the rejection of two suggestions about what knowledge is, and the partial rejection of a third.

The first point Plato makes is that the question is not 'What sort of things do we know?', but 'What is it to know something?', 'What is knowledge?' To give examples of things that are known will not do. A general answer is needed.

The first suggestion is that knowledge is perception. But mathematical knowledge is not perception, although it may initially have to be elicited by sight or touch. Most things are indeed discovered by perception. For example, I find out by seeing or hearing that something is the case at 7.15 am today, but I know it until memory fails. Perception by itself is not knowledge. It is the source of the river, not the river itself.

The second suggestion is that knowledge is true belief – or, in other words, that to know is to believe and be right. There is much discussion in the *Theaetetus* about what false judgment or false belief is, but the nub of the matter is that true belief and knowledge are different things. An orator or preacher may persuade me to believe what happens to be true, but I cannot legitimately claim to know what he has persuaded me. It is certainly worth having a true belief rather than a false one, but a false belief would still be a belief. False knowledge would not be knowledge at all.

The third suggestion Theaetetus makes is that knowledge is true belief with a *logos*. As I have said before, *logos* is a word with many meanings. Plato himself excludes some, and translators differ, but for its use in the *Theaetetus* the best authorities usually give 'statement' or 'reason'. So Plato's final suggestion is that knowledge is true belief with a reason.

The dialogue concludes with Plato – in the character of Socrates – making an attempt to distinguish what had never before been distinguished: the difference between words, sentences and meanings. In short, he finishes with an analysis of what a statement is. (You may begin to appreciate the difficulty if you know that ancient Greek was always written as a continuous string of letters without word gaps or punctuation.) In the end, all Socrates claims is to have pricked a few 'wind bubbles' (his own words) in order to achieve a little better understanding of the matter. There is no dogmatic conclusion.

2 **The two-worlds answer.** Plato's analytic answer to the question 'What is knowledge?' demands exacting attention and critical skills − as I'm afraid you may have noticed. The two-world answer is presented with reasons and persuasive arguments, but it is made intuitively vivid in the best-known metaphor in all philosophical literature. It is the metaphor of the cave, given at the beginning of Book VII of the *Republic*. Here it is, abbreviated, but almost entirely in Plato's own words:

> Let me show you in a picture how far our nature is enlightened or unenlightened. Behold, human beings are housed in a long cave which has an entrance towards the light. They have been chained since childhood so that they can only see the back of the cave, and never turn to the light or see each other. Behind them, outside the cave and at a distance, a great fire is blazing. Immediately outside the cave is a path with a low wall between it and the cave entrance. And do you see free men passing along the path carrying all sorts of things which appear over the wall, like the screen which marionette players have in front of them, over which they show the puppets?
> − I see.
> The prisoners are like ourselves, I replied, for in the first place do you think they have seen anything of themselves, and of one another, except the shadows which the fire throws on the back wall of the cave?
> − How could they do so, he asked, if throughout their lives they were never allowed to move their heads?

And of the objects that were being carried by free men the other side of the wall, the prisoners would, in like manner, see only the shadows at the back of the cave?

– Yes, he said.

And if they were able to converse with one another, would they not apply the word 'real' to the shadows which they see?

– Very true.

And suppose further that the prison had an echo which came from the back, would they not be sure to fancy, when one of the passers-by spoke, that the voice which they heard came from the shadow at the back of the cave?

– No question, he replied.

To them, I said, the truth would be literally nothing but the shadows of the realities they could not turn to see.

The picture is clear: we experience the shadows of what is real. It needs thought and understanding to perceive that things are mere images, and that the real forms of things have another existence.

Plato – always through the voice of Socrates, so there may be some genuine Socratic origin to the idea – urges the two worlds repeatedly, picturesquely and with reasons, the most powerful of which comes from an account of how general names get their meaning – an account he implicitly uses in his quests for definitions of love, fairness, beauty, and so on.

We easily understand how particular or proper names work. John Gaskin is the name of the man to whose words you are now, I trust, attending. It 'means' me. Mrs Squeezeaweezle is the name of the woman who fell out of the bus yesterday. But 'cat' is not (normally) the name of any particular cat. It is some sort of general name applicable in countless instances. How does this work? Plato's answer is that 'cat' is the particular or proper name of some real entity – the ideal form of a cat – and all lesser, shadow-world, this-world, actual cats in our experience are only able to be called cats because they are like, or approximate in various ways to, the ideal form of a cat. Then comes the big jump: the ideal form exists in another world of full realities. All right, cats are to some people of limited intellectual interest. They can't count beyond about five, for instance, and they have very few moral sensibilities. It is mathematical concepts and moral or aesthetic abstracts such as beauty, good and justice that best fit and illustrate Plato's theory of ideal forms.

Consider geometry: a line is defined as that which has length but no breadth. No such thing could be drawn. It couldn't even be seen. In this case, the fuzzy mark on the paper is manifestly only an attempt, a shadow, of the thing defined. In politics and social life we all too often call something 'fair' or 'unfair'. But the things so named are multifarious, sometimes wildly different; Plato would say that we need to find the best definition of fairness that we can, and that will give us a description, an idea, of the form of fairness that actually exists in the other world. Through their similarity with this ideal form of fairness, all the things we call 'fair' in this world are justifiably called 'fair'.

In conclusion, to know the ideal forms of things, and in particular to know the form of the good, is to have knowledge; and Plato (Socrates?) hopes and expects that the other world of ideal forms will become directly accessible to us when we survive death as intellectual souls and can see the perfect realities themselves.

Accept it or not, Plato's two-world theory was of incalculable influence. It is the core of the metaphysic that gives rational structure to Christian and Islamic accounts of God, heaven and an afterlife, and it is taken for granted in much of what we think and say. It was subjected to devastating criticism by Aristotle; it is contrary to the one-world structure of Epicureanism and Stoicism; it is alien to the ideas of modern science. But it persists.

* * *

To read further into the philosophy of Plato is a serious undertaking. A relatively easy start can be made in *Socrates: A Very Short Introduction* (Oxford, revd edn 2000) by C. C. W. Taylor. Some of Plato's own early works are quite easy – the *Charmides, Lysis* and the *Laches*, for instance. The four dialogues concerning the death of Socrates are harder, but still manageable. Some of the articles in *The Cambridge Companion to Plato* (ed. Richard Kraut; Cambridge, 1992) are helpful.

Plato (holding his ideal under his arm) being teased by Aristotle.

6

Aristotle and this World: Nature, Life and Ethics

'They have left behind them compilations such as no one can bear to read to the end.' Dionysius of Halicarnassus (*c.* 30 BC – after AD 8) was not writing about Aristotle, but in the experience of generations of students he might well have been. The scale and profundity of Aristotle's intellectual and practical learning, as both scientist and philosopher, have no parallel in the history of human achievement. He is quite simply the cleverest man who ever lived, and his thought is inordinately difficult to give an account of without having the reader glaze over and reach for something easy like *War and Peace*. Even Aristotle himself might have sympathized. In the *Problems,* a kind of notebook of questions as they occurred to him, he asks: 'Why is it that in some cases, if men begin to read, they are overtaken by sleep against their will, while it makes others keep awake, even when they want to sleep, when they take up a book?' I don't know of any adequate and easily read book on Aristotle – that's why none are recommended at the end of this chapter. But he is the greatest philosopher of the ancient world, and if the ideas of such a man – many still viable today – do not justify a little effort, then indeed we sleep and nothing matters.

Life and works

All Aristotle's early works, written under the influence of Plato, are lost; so are all those he prepared for publication (the easy stuff!). What survives are his own or his students' lecture notes, records of field trips and dissections, tightly argued treatises, and short, probing examinations of particular subjects. In translation these fill about eleven modern printed books. He is the first systematic marine biologist, and for more than two thousand years the best. He invented logic. He was in most instances the first to construct major works that separated the subjects of ethics, politics, aesthetics, physics, metaphysics (or 'first philosophy', as he called it), cosmology, meteorology, rhetoric, zoology, the philosophy of mind, and on the vexed question 'What is life?' It is scarcely surprising that Plato referred to the approach of his best pupil in terms like 'Here comes the Brain'.

Aristotle was born in the minor city of Stageira, on the peninsula of Chalcidice, in 384 BC. His father was court physician to the grandfather of Alexander the Great, a connection of momentous importance. In 367, when he was 17, he migrated to Athens to join the teaching institution already established by Plato and known as the Academy. After the death of Plato in 347, Aristotle left Athens to live at Assos. He then moved to Mytilene on the nearby island of Lesbos, where the two lagoons, teaming with marine life, were the location for his biological investigations, undertaken alongside another outstanding philosopher–scientist, Theophrastus (a few years Aristotle's junior).

In 343 Philip II of Macedonia summoned Aristotle to his capital, Pella (north-west of Thessalonica), to become tutor to the 13-year-old Alexander. In 340 Alexander became regent, and Aristotle was free to return to Athens, where he established his own teaching institution – the Lyceum – in about 335. If the Academy during its founder's lifetime could best be regarded as a club where learned gentlemen could discuss and where youths could learn, then the Lyceum could be called a research institute. Empirical science and theoretical analysis were pursued at a high level. The lectures were open to anyone. Biological specimens were collected and books accumulated.

Having conquered the known world from the Danube to the Indus, Alexander the Great, erstwhile pupil and enduring patron of Aristotle, died in 323. In the outburst of anti-Macedonian feeling in Athens after his death, Aristotle deemed it prudent to leave with his wife and family lest the Athenians, as he put it, 'sin twice against philosophy'. He died a year later.

The garrulous Diogenes Laertius reproduces Aristotle's will – kind to family and slaves alike – and a catalogue of his written works. He also provides a few 'happy sayings' of the sort: 'What do people gain by telling lies? Not being believed when they tell the truth.' What he does not attempt is any account of Aristotle's thought. Can we fill a few parts of this gap?

Biology

The bulk of Aristotle's scientific fieldwork was conducted while he was residing at Assos and on Lesbos. It is serious research – the collecting, describing and dissection of species and their classification. He identified 495 species. The descriptions are precise and illuminating, and the dissections careful and thorough. In his several texts on the subject of biology, he includes work on the human body, which he treats as no more than that of a particularly interesting animal with considerable similarities to other living things. As he says, 'We should approach the investigation of every kind of animal without embarrassment, for each will show us something natural and something beautiful.' His *Enquiry into Animals* (the Greek word translated as 'enquiry' is *historia*, meaning information obtained through investigation) is a weighty gathering of data, including detailed information about insects and fish. His other works on biology develop theory from observation, and include studies on the parts of animals, their movement and reproduction.

It is not Aristotle's fault if his work was so good that nobody corrected his mistakes for the better part of two thousand years. One error – not addressed until the 20th century AD – was in concluding that eels had no genitalia and formed spontaneously in the mud. That the European eel developed genitalia on its way to the far side of the Atlantic and spawned in the Sargasso Sea could scarcely have been established by observation, however minute, carried out in the Aegean. Another, absurdly enduring mistake was Aristotle's conclusion that maggots formed in and from putrefying fluids. Again, he was blamed for what nobody bothered to correct simply by having another look – a delay of some eighteen centuries.

Aristotle's scientific curiosity does not stop at observation and description. He always wants to explain at the deepest level possible why things are as they are. That leads him to ask what life is, and what counts as an explanation.

Explanation

In the book on logic called the *Posterior* ('later') *Analytics*, Aristotle gives a detailed account of something that many of his commentators call 'scientific method'. But it is not what he himself uses. The *Analytics* sets out a structure in which a certain type of knowledge can be presented.

The structure was best exemplified in ancient times by Euclid's geometry, produced shortly after Aristotle's death; it is a deductive system in which, once certain things are taken as given and definitions have been made, the rest follows according to logical rules.

A better account of what Aristotle himself did is in the *Physics*. The first concern is to establish that empirical observation is the source of knowledge: 'If we did not perceive anything we would not learn or understand anything.' But the observation must be examined. If we honestly claim to see white, then we do. But we may be mistaken in saying that we see a white thing. The sensation cannot be other than it is, but it can misinterpret. Look more closely: what we see could be brilliant sunshine reflecting off a shiny black surface, not a white thing. Such carefully checked observation is the bedrock of scientific knowledge. Once it has been established, it can be categorized and may fit into a general theory. In cases where observation is deemed to be insufficient, Aristotle has the right modern prescription: 'The facts have not yet been sufficiently ascertained,' (he has been talking about bees) 'and if at any future time they are ascertained, then credence must be given to the direct evidence of the senses rather than to theories, and to theories also, provided that the results which they generate agree with what is observed' (*Generation of Animals* III.10). So what is it to give an explanation of something when we have facts and workable theories?

The four 'causes'

According to Aristotle, the 'how and why' of things that change is provided by giving an account of four *aitia*. This word is usually translated as 'causes', but that sets up the wrong expectations. Let's call them four explanations. They are set out in Book II of the *Physics*, and are as follows:

1 **The material explanation.** This offers an account of what the stuff is from which the thing has been made. The jug is made of silver. The lake is made of water. The water is made of hydrogen and oxygen. Hydrogen is made of ... .

2 **The formal explanation.** 'Then the thing in question cannot be there unless the material has actually received the form or

characteristic of the type, conformity to which brings it within the definition of the thing we say it is.' The formal explanation is the pattern, shape or formula that must be satisfied before the thing can be what we say it is. The silver must be in a certain form before the thing can be a jug. It can't just be a blob of metal. The lake must have shoreline boundaries. It can't just be a boundless expanse of water.

3 **The efficient explanation.** 'There must be something to initiate the process of change' – to produce the thing – 'or its cessation when the process is completed, such as the act of a voluntary agent' – of the smith, for instance, who made the jug; or the slow-moving process of geological change that brought about the lake. This is as near as we get in Aristotle to the still somewhat fuzzy modern notion of causation, according to which something originates or 'produces' something new and distinct from itself.

4 **The 'final purpose' explanation.** 'There is the end or purpose, for the sake of which the process is initiated, as when a man takes exercise for the sake of his health' – or the purpose of the silversmith in making the jug. This is the element in the explanation of an object that so appealed to the medieval world in its desire to see God's purposes in all creation. Today we are more inclined to say that not all things have purposes. Obviously most human activities and artefacts do. But what is the purpose of a meteorite? Not much. It is still difficult, however, to avoid the language of purpose in the life sciences: we say, for example, 'The salmon goes up river in order to spawn', even though the salmon, with its somewhat limited intelligence, does not comprehend what it is doing.

So when with any particular object of enquiry we have identified the four explanations (or three, if the fourth cannot be found), we understand the 'how and the why' of a thing as well as we can. But if we search into efficient explanations, pressing the quest back and back, an intellectual problem of strange importance is encountered.

Aristotle's 'God'

Aristotle did not have the problem of explaining the origin of the universe because, together with all his Classical predecessors and successors, he took it to be eternal, given for always, and hence not having an explanation. However, if we ask for the efficient explanation of some particular movement or change (movement and change are often treated as interchangeable in Greek philosophical writing), we find ourselves always referring back to some previous movement or change. Now, Aristotle argues (and the argument is much more complex than I shall make it seem) that, in order to stop an infinite series of movements or changes, we must suppose something that is unmoved by any other thing. Such an entity could only be outside, or different in kind from, the moved universe. If it were a part of the moved universe, then it would itself move and be moved. But in order not to be a part of the moved universe, it must lack matter, be no kind of stuff that changes, and hence not come into existence or go out of existence or become something else. So IT is an eternal, motionless being of which we can say (without understanding) that IT thinks or knows itself. And this entity (Aristotle often refers to the divine in the neuter singular) is called God. IT is the efficient reason for, or explanation of, why the universe moves rather than remains in motionless silence for ever.

An objection will occur to you almost at once. If the universe of space and stuff – whatever the stuff is – can be an eternal inexplicable given, why shouldn't its movement be part of that given? This is the route to be taken by the Epicureans shortly after Aristotle's death, but it is not the one taken by Christian and Islamic theologians. They adapted and adopted Aristotle's thought concerning the origin of motion into a favoured argument for the existence of God – their God. But their conclusion is estranged from Aristotle in two ways. The first is that Aristotle never uses IT to proclaim monotheism. For him, IT is the end of an intellectual quest, during which he has left all the ordinary gods, to whom he refers without hesitation, in place. Second, IT would not be interested in forgiving a sinner or providing a paradise for the martyr. Awesome IT may be; concerned with life, and us in particular, IT is not. As we shall see, for Aristotle life is simply a part of nature, and we are no more than a part of that part.

Life is having a 'soul'

The question 'What is it that something has that entitles us to say it lives?' occupies Aristotle's attention in one of his profoundest and, until recently, least appreciated works – the *De anima*, or 'On the Soul' (the Latin title is generally used). It was written well after his sojourn on Lesbos, but the question must have formed itself in view of the curious objects he identified and described there. His answer, in deceptive brevity, is that life is having a soul, a *psuche*, not as an extra, independent or detachable part of a living thing, but as a certain sort of function and organization within the thing that is said to live.

A note of warning: the Greek word *psuche* (Latin *anima*) is conventionally translated into English as 'soul'. But because of its use in two thousand years of Christianity, and the meaning it therefore normally carries in English, the translation 'soul' tends to decide the very question Aristotle is asking. To us, the soul is the non-bodily entity – whether we believe in it or not – that can survive death. It is the *me* independent of this mortal shell. In some Greek philosophical accounts – notably those of Plato and the Pythagoreans – this is indeed the meaning *psuche* is given. In others, in particular the account of Epicurus, it is not. Aristotle is trying to decide the issue. Despite the damaged and defective text, his analysis (mainly in Books II and III of *De anima*) is a wonderful example of the way he pushes the questioning back behind superficial words, and on behind the words used to explain words. In short measure, his account, given as far as possible in his own words, is this:

'That which has soul is distinguished from that which has not by life.' This means that an oyster, a mushroom, a fly, a human being, a tree, and anything that lives will have a soul of some sort.

If we say that a thing lives because it has a soul, is this to say that the thing and its soul are two entities? No. 'We should not ask whether the body and soul are one [or two], any more than whether the wax and the impression it receives are one [or two].' Similarly, 'just as the pupil and sight make up the eye, so body and soul make up a living creature ... And for this reason those are right who maintain that the soul cannot exist without the body, but is not in itself any kind of body. It is not a body. It is something which belongs to a body.' And that belonging thing called 'the soul' is the form and function an entity must have in order to be said to live.

The background argument, which I have largely ignored, is complex, but the outcome is decisive: 'It is quite evident that the soul, or certain parts of it, if it has parts, cannot be separated from the body.' But Aristotle, perhaps with an eye still cast back at his master Plato, has one hesitation: 'Concerning the intellect and the capacity for contemplation nothing is yet clear. It seems to be a distinct kind of soul, and this alone can exist separately.'

What is having a soul?

So life is having a soul, and a soul is the form and function of something that entitles us to say that the thing lives. What is this form and function? Aristotle's answer is that it is to have all or some of the following: 'intellect, perception, movement and rest in respect of place, and that motion implied in nutrition and decay or growth'. His answer leads him to an analysis of sense perception, to the identification of touch as the most basic of the senses (the lowest forms of life, even plants, respond in some ways to touch) and on to the highly general philosophical question 'What is perception?' His answer is famous: 'In general, with regard to sense perception, we must take it that a sense is that which can receive the form of the sensible object without its matter, just as the wax receives the impression of the signet ring without the iron or the gold; receiving the impression of the gold or bronze, but not *as* gold or bronze.'

Aristotle appears to be in doubt on the question of whether the mind or intellect is a separable part of the highly complex soul that humans must have in order to live. But in a sentence that anticipates the modern philosophy of mind by twenty-three centuries, he appears to emerge from the shadow of Plato: 'That part of the soul which we call mind – by mind I mean that part of the soul which thinks and forms judgments – has no actual existence until it thinks.' This appears to be saying that thinking is one among the functions that make up the human soul, and like the other functions it will not exist when it is not functioning – before it develops or after death, for example. Mind is not a detachable *thing* of any sort.

In a similar manner, earlier in the *De anima* – and in contradiction to Descartes' now infamous 'ghost in the machine' idea – Aristotle implies that the mind is not a thing pulling levers in the body from whatever physical location we give it. It is a function that only highly developed living things perform: 'It is uncertain whether the soul … bears the same relation to the body as the captain to the ship.'

The implication of all this is that, for Aristotle (as perhaps for many who live in the world now), personal immortality is not a possibility commended by reason. No part of the soul, even the intellect, is obviously other than a function or potential of the living body. For human beings, therefore – as Homer's heroes understood – life is all we have, and living in the best possible way is of supreme importance. So what is that way? As before, with Aristotle the landscape is wide; our peep at it no more than a glimpse of the Parthenon from afar.

Ethics and how to live

In speaking about morality (and some of us still do), we tend to think about commandments, obligations, duties, the will of God, prohibitions (whether divine or human), punishment (whether divine or human) and forgiveness (whether divine or human). In Aristotle's two major works, the *Nicomachean Ethics* – named after his son Nicomachus – and the *Eudemian Ethics*, the word 'ethics' means matters concerning character, and his investigation is refreshingly different from what we would expect. It includes such questions as, What life is best to lead? What makes for happiness? What freedom do we need to be responsible for our actions? How can we form our characters in such a way as to be successful human beings? In his answers there is virtually no talk about rules, duties or moral laws.

Aristotle opens with the question, What is it we desire for its own sake, and not as a means to something else? 'Verbally,' he says, 'there is very general agreement; … (people) identify living well and doing well with being happy, but with regard to what happiness is they differ.' So, ignoring for the moment what happiness is, what is it to live a satisfactory and successful life?

The beginning of an answer to that question is that the good life is practising virtue. Oh dear, how unexciting! But the word being translated as 'virtue' (I've said this sort of thing before, but the translation alters everything) is *arete*, which means skill or excellence at something. So you might have the *arete* required to do crosswords, while I might have the *arete* to catch wasps. Aristotle is asking what the *arete* to live successfully is. For once his arguments are relatively easy to explain.

The skill of living successfully consists of developing a character that as a habit chooses the right action. The right action, according to Aristotle, is in many instances the mean between two extremes, both of which are defects. Some examples: at one extremity is rashness, and at the other craven cowardice, but somewhere in the middle is courage appropriate to the circumstances and your own limitations. Likewise, at one extremity are vanity, conceit and snobbery, and at the other excessive humility and self-deprecation; the mean is self-respect, and in that sense proper pride. Or, finally, in a case where one extremity would be giving all you have to the poor, and the other keeping everything you have all the time, the mean would be something like giving a proportion suited to your means.

How do we find the mean? Partly by thinking, partly by observing how the successful human being behaves. But the mean will not always be the same in all circumstances. It is a practical thing. The skill required to discover what it is can be learnt, and, for the successful person, using it will become a habit, part of their character, just as a bricklayer or a car driver has practical skills that are habitually employed but adjusted to the needs of the task in hand without worrying thought or painful choices.

Note, however, that 'not every action or passion admits of a mean'. Some have 'names that already imply badness', and any character in which these feature as passions or actions will not be successful, will not achieve life's ultimate objective, happiness. Among defective passions Aristotle lists spite, shamelessness and envy: for these there is no happy mean. Among actions he lists adultery, theft and murder, where likewise no mean is possible. They just never feature in the successful life.

What are the conditions for the happiness that goes with the successful life? One is activity. Happiness accompanies the successfully completed task, not the inertia of the Lotus-Eater. However trivial or magnificent, successfully undertaken activity – be it growing potatoes, writing a book, attending to a piece of music, going for a walk or offering hospitality – is accompanied by happiness. Another condition is having at least a minimum of material possessions. To put it negatively, *not* being continually ill, grindingly poor, hideously ugly or deprived of all one's friends, relatives and material goods is required for real happiness. Such deprivations can be endured by the wise, but they are inimical to normal life and hence to happiness. In sum, 'he is happy who is active in accordance with complete *arete*, and is sufficiently equipped with external goods, not for some chance period, but throughout a complete life.'

Voluntary acts and responsible acts

There is no need to go beyond Aristotle's own words at the beginning of Book III of the *Nicomachean Ethics* to see the point of his worry:

> Since *arete* is concerned with passions and actions, and only on voluntary passions and actions are praise and blame bestowed, while those that are involuntary are condoned, and sometimes also pitied – to distinguish the voluntary and the involuntary is presumably necessary for those who are studying the nature of *arete*, and also useful for legislators with a view to assigning both honours and punishments.

He then sets the standard for what we might call the 'tough' definition of what is involuntary.

Involuntary acts are those that take place under compulsion or owing to ignorance. They are acts whose 'moving principle is outside the person, … and in which nothing is contributed by the person who is acting or feeling the passion' – as when one is physically forced by men or natural conditions, including the condition of one's own body. Very sensibly, Aristotle points out that there is a 'mixed case' that affects praise and blame. I pay a ransom to a criminal to save my child, but I am not under bodily compulsion: 'Such actions are voluntary, but in the circumstances are perhaps involuntary, for no one would choose to do any such thing in itself.'

But how does choice relate to what is voluntary? (Notice how Aristotle never tries to solve a problem with an idea that leaves problems unsolved.) They are not the same thing. 'Acts done on the spur of the moment we describe as voluntary, but not as chosen.' And again, 'acts done from anger are thought to be less than any others objects of choice.' Choice requires previous deliberation; voluntary acts do not.

The applications of these definitions are sane and viable. The voluntary action done on impulse is less blameworthy (and conversely less praiseworthy) than the action chosen after consideration. The 'mixed-case' voluntary action – when we feel compelled, but are not forced, to do what we would not choose to do – is excusable. The person who is so mentally imperfect that they have no means to stop themselves attacking someone is undertaking an involuntary act requiring pardon, and also pity.

In ethics Aristotle, as so often in his writings, combines that rare thing, practical common sense, with an altogether extraordinary ability to make new distinctions, ask original questions and pursue problems into the undergrowth. Do look at least at the first few pages of Books I and III of the *Nicomachean Ethics* to get a flavour of the original. All I have tried to show is how stimulatingly different and non-moralistic Aristotle's account of the good life is. It is entirely of this world, and concerned with living a life good for oneself, and good to be observed by others – which again may be good for us in terms of public approval. If we are really good at living, we may even expect to teach others by our example.

The way leads on

The death of Alexander the Great in 323 BC marks the beginning of what historians call the Hellenistic Age (the Hellenic, on the other hand, covers everything Greek from Homer to about the 4th century AD). It is the period when the divided segments of Alexander's empire were ruled by his generals and their successors, and when Hellenic influence in culture, language, philosophy, buildings and civic organization spread all over the lands of the eastern Mediterranean. The period's end is sometimes understood as 146 BC, when Rome took control of mainland Greece, but more usually as 30 BC, when the death of Cleopatra ended the rule of the last Egyptian descendent of Alexander's general Ptolemy Soter, and Rome became master of the whole Mediterranean area. The Hellenistic Age, then, is roughly 323 to 30 BC.

Aristotle died the year after Alexander, but within thirty years Athens was buzzing with philosophies, and, in the new city of Alexandria, Ptolemy I and his son had established the great library and the museum, a well-endowed research institute. In Athens, Plato's

Academy continued, the Lyceum was re-established by Aristotle's talented pupil and colleague Theophrastus, and new schools of philosophy were formed that eventually attracted the elite of Rome to finish their education there.

The greatest and most enduring of the various new teaching institutions that sprang up in Athens after the death of Aristotle were that of the Stoics, established by Zeno of Citium, who came to Athens in 313 BC (not to be confused with Zeno of the paradoxes), and that of the Epicureans, set up by Epicurus in about 306. By the 1st century BC, both philosophies were known and taught widely in the Roman Empire. Both had an influence that endures to the present day: Stoicism as admirable fortitude, and Epicureanism as the origin of the atomic theory and as fastidious self-indulgence. There is vastly more to both; but as far as it goes the modern idea of Stoicism is right, while the modern view of Epicureanism is a travesty, originating in early Christian misrepresentation of a system that challenged the new religion as a way of life, and differed from it in every possible way as an account of the natural universe.

7

Epicurus:
The Garden and the Wilderness

The atomic theory is the foundation of modern science. Most people do not know how ancient it is, and how well developed it was before it was rubbished by theologians and philosophers, and buried until the 17th century AD. Its origins can be traced back to the shadowy figure of Leucippus, possibly from Miletus, and it was perhaps an offspring of the physicalist speculations about nature that began in that city in the 6th century BC. Almost nothing is known about Leucippus, but both Aristotle and Theophrastus identify him as the originator of atomism. One sentence asserting what we would now call determinism survives from his book *The Great World System*: 'Nothing happens at random, but everything from a scientific principle and of necessity.'

It is, however, to the less remote Democritus of Abdera (*c.* 460–*c.* 370 BC) that we can trace the first details of ancient deterministic atomism. His writings, had they survived, would in length rival those of Plato. But even with him all we have are scraps and quotations, from which we can discern someone capable of wise and witty remarks about human life, and one who worked out a deterministic account of nature in terms of the existence, movement and combination of invisible particles. Epicurus (341–*c.* 270 BC) gave us the account of atomism as *random* movements of particles, in which he was followed by the Roman poet Lucretius (*c.* 98–*c.* 55 BC), whose great book, *De rerum natura* ('On the nature of the universe'), was held in being for us by the chance survival of a single manuscript.

Epicurus was born on the island of Samos as an Athenian citizen. In 323 he went to Athens to do his two years' military and civic service for the city. He then probably lived for a period in Colophon, in Mytilene on Lesbos, and then in Lampsacus on the coast of Asia Minor, just before the Hellespont opens out into the Sea of Marmara. He returned to Athens in about 306, and stayed there for the rest of his life, teaching, writing and establishing 'the Garden' – the community outside the city walls that carried forward his name and teaching.

The Garden was not like the Academy or the Lyceum: it was not a college, club or research institute, but rather a society of friends living according to the principles of Epicurus, in semi-isolation from civic society. Its teachings and way of life spread. By the 1st century BC communities existed in many parts of the Roman world, from Gadara, south-east of the Sea of Galilee, to Naples and Gaul. Even Julius Caesar was reputed to have had Epicurean sympathies.

Epicurus' most important work, *On Nature*, is lost, although parts of it are being painstakingly reconstructed from carbonized papyrus rolls found at Herculaneum. Three letters, his brief *Principal Doctrines*, a cluster of sayings and his will survive. We have a complete statement of his philosophy and physics only in Lucretius, together with partial developments in works (again being retrieved from Herculaneum) by Philodemus of Gadara, and – unique in the entire world as a philosophical document – in the surviving parts of the immense stone inscription erected in Oinoanda by one Diogenes in about AD 130.

One-world systems: Epicurean and Stoic

The Epicureans and their rivals the Stoics shared just one very general view of reality. They both advocated what can be called 'one-world' philosophies. The Pythagoreans, the Platonists, the Christians and, by the 3rd century AD, the Gnostics and Neoplatonists all espoused two- (or more!) world philosophies, distinguishing between body and soul, this world and the next world, the perishing body and the immortal body, matter and spirit, and the natural and the supernatural. In contrast, for the Epicureans and Stoics all that is real is, or is a part of, a single universe in which the contrast between matter and spirit is meaningless. This is not to say that either school was obliged to deny the existence of gods, or the experiences or phenomena we call 'spiritual'. It is just that they both – in different ways – say that those things, if they exist, are parts or functions of one all-embracing universal system, not two.

The two schools also shared a method of organizing and presenting their ideas. Both developed a logic that makes possible the exposition of a physics, which in turn implies a right way of living: an ethic. They began with an account of language, logic and what we can know – the Stoic account being vastly better than the Epicurean. They follow this with what we might call scientific accounts of the nature of reality: the physics. The Epicurean account is closer to the chemistry and particle physics that it helped to originate; the Stoic, as we shall see in the next chapter, is closer to Big Bang cosmology and the idea of a dynamically evolving universe. Given that each school claims to have provided a true account of physical reality (the word 'physical' is redundant, since there is no other sort of reality with which to contrast the physical), how should we live? Both ethical prescriptions are attractive. (As for the logic, let me at once disappoint you: there is no room here for its intricacies.)

The Epicurean physics

The foundation of the system is that the universe – the 'all viewed as one' – has two real constituents: body and void space. The existence of body is proved to us by sensation; if we cannot know by sensation that there are bodies, then we cannot know anything at all. But bodies have location, and they move. That is to say, the universe is not as it might have been – solid, packed tight, immobile. In brief: 'All nature … is built of those two things: for there are bodies, and there is the void in which they are placed and where they move' (Lucretius, *De rerum natura*, Book I). The Epicurean contention is that the occurrence and working of bodies in space – all of them, including, eventually, ourselves – can be accounted for by the existence and movement of an infinite number of irreducibly tiny particles, for which the Greek language provided the name *atomoi*, 'uncuttables', and the Latin *primordia*, 'first things'.

The *atomoi* or *primordia* may well be of a limited range of sizes, but all are too small to be seen. Their existence can be inferred only from what can be seen, and they can be used to explain the things that we do see. They are everlasting, they contain no void within themselves, they cannot be split or divided, and they move.

Why should anyone think of matter as made up of particles no one could ever see? In the background lies the Greek inclination to look behind surface appearances for explanations; in the particular case of the particles proposed by Democritus and Epicurus, the fact of their existence was arrived at explicitly through the questioning of common observations. For example, how is it that two objects of identical volume, say a cube of gold and a cube of marble, weigh differently? It could be that one has more, or larger, particles packed into its apparent solidity than the other. Or again: we may notice normally invisible motes in a sunbeam, and infer from this the existence of even smaller bodies that we cannot see. Another reason for the particle hypothesis is that it provides a way of explaining things. Solids, for instance, could be composed of particles clogged together in virtue of their shapes; fluids of smoother or less densely packed particles; and air of even finer particles that slip over each other with very little stickiness. The attrition of hard objects by soft – coins rubbed by fingers, steps worn down by feet – without the visible disappearance of any part might be explained by the loss of imperceptible particles.

Why are there primary particles? Simply because there are. They exist as an ultimate fact about reality much as for some people God exists. For Epicurus, to ask why there are primary particles is foolishness, because the question tries to look outside all that really exists for an explanation of what exists, and nothing exists outside all that exists. But the primary particles do not merely exist, they move. They 'wander through the void'. They 'move of themselves'. The problem of Aristotle's 'unmoved mover' is thus solved. He accepted the stuff of the universe as eternal, not needing or having an explanation, but sought an explanation of its movement. Epicurus takes it that matter and its movement are not separable: they are together part of the given.

Yet the particles move in a particular way – not guidedly, or in a deterministic manner, as Democritus supposed, but randomly. According to Epicurus, the particles swerve or alter direction in such a way that no prior knowledge of the particles and their movements could ever give knowledge of when and in what manner any given particle will change direction. The outcome of such particle swerves would be chaos: an infinite number of random collisions taking place eternally. How, then, does this chaos of primary particles result in the ordered cosmos we experience all the time? Epicurus has a sort of answer. It is this.

Particles come in a large but finite number of variations of size and shape. The modern idea of elements might help to convey the idea.

The shapes of the various sorts of particles limit the ways they can link up with other particles when collisions take place. Primordial collisions and movements are chaotic, but the successful and semi-enduring unions that take place are not. These produce everything from suns to grains of sand, and us. Things we can sense are thus the result of the primary particles' different combining powers, or 'stickiness'.

There is an obvious gap in this account. Once the chaos of particles has produced things and categories of things, the things behave according to regularities we call the 'laws of nature'. Most of these laws are not readily explicable in terms of the movement and combination of primary particles. Or are they? The Stoics thought not. For us, the jury is still out.

To sum up: the whole universe is comprehended within two natures, void space and primary particles in random motion. The universe is eternal. The motion and combinations of the primary particles account for all that happens, and all sensible bodies that exist, and for sensation itself. (Epicurus' account maintains that things emit surface particles that strike our sense organs, causing sight, hearing, etc.)

Epicurean physics: The consequences for humanity
There are three consequences of Epicurean physics that touch very closely upon human life and hopes. Epicurus was fully aware of them.

The first is that, very probably, neither we nor the earth are unique. If particles and space are infinite, they will produce the same things more than once: other earths, with other or the same creatures on them, will exist. The human race is not alone; but neither are we the result of any purposeful evolution of primary particles. Neither this nor any other world was made by God, or gods, for our convenience. We thus have no significance beyond that which we give ourselves: no final purpose, no metaphysical or religious objective. We and our world are like all other things. We form, we grow, we decay and return to the universe's primordial store of particles. Lucretius – the verses are a paraphrase from Book II – describes the process thus:

> Nothing abides. The seas in minute haze
> Depart; those moonèd sands forsake their place;
> And where they are shall other seas in turn
> Mow with their scythes of whiteness other bays.

The antipathy of the early (and later!) Christians to this species of Hellenistic philosophy will cause little surprise, but there is worse to come.

The second consequence of the Epicurean physics is that either God and gods do not exist, or they are parts of the universe of void space and moving particles. Perhaps out of a real piety towards the multitude of gods with which his culture surrounded him – or perhaps because he recognized their importance as the focus for civic, and later imperial, ceremony, loyalty and identity – Epicurus subscribed to the latter view. In so doing, he required the gods to be described in a way that would become offensively unacceptable to religion. The gods exist as bodies of unobservably fine particles in space. They are forever happy, inactive, self-sufficient, and totally without concern for us or knowledge of us. Lucretius again, in Book III of *De rerum natura*:

> At ease they dream, and make perpetual cheer
> Far off. From them we nothing have to fear:
> And nothing hope. How should the calm ones hate?
> The tearless, know the meaning of a tear?

Their only value to us is to provide some example of the sort of happy life to which we might remotely aspire.

The third consequence of the Epicurean physics, but also backed up by numerous other arguments in Lucretius, is that no human being can survive bodily death, the break up of the structure of particles that is the individual. Mind and life are complex parts or movements of the briefly existing structures of primary particles that constitute you and me. That is all. Since the mind moves the body – we experience this – it must in some sense be touching it, connected with it as part of the same structure. The mind no more survives the corruption of the physical body than the scent of a rose can outlive the rotting of the bloom. Here, for the last time, is Lucretius in his great poem:

> Observe this dew-drenched rose of Tyrian hue –
> A rose today. But you will ask in vain
> Tomorrow what it is; and yesterday
> It was the dust, the sunshine and the rain.
> Where is the coolness when no cool winds blow?

Where is the music when the lute lies low?
Are not the redness and the red rose one,
And the snow's whiteness one thing with the snow?

In Book III of *De rerum natura*, Lucretius goes far beyond any arguments for mortality known to have been set out by Epicurus himself. The whole section is a concentrated presentation of almost all the arguments and evidence – metaphysical, physical, moral and psychological – for the mortality of the soul that have ever been assembled. Why are mortality and its glad acceptance advocated so fervently by Lucretius, and more prosaically by Epicurus? Because acceptance of mortality removes mankind's fear of the one absolute certainty of human existence – death – and thus provides one of the conditions for living well.

The way of life
In bare outline, the Epicurean prescription for the good life is simple. It is the happy life, and happiness is living in peaceful friendship and good relations with others, a body free from pain of whatever kind, and a mind free from fear and anxiety.

Living among friends, and how to do so from the point of view of the individual, was a cardinal concern of Epicurus – hence his founding of the Garden, a community of like-minded people living in amicable cooperation. And for Epicurus (as, later, for the early Christians), 'people' meant anyone who would live in accordance with the teaching – men, women and slaves without social distinction.

The friendship, *philia*, that Epicurus advocated is sometimes translated 'love'. But Greek, unlike English, has three words for love: *eros*, meaning sexual love; *philia*, meaning the friendship possible between any human beings without regard to sex; and *agape*, a somewhat rarified concept usually rendered as 'spiritual love'. Perhaps one can have spiritual love for a dead saint or even for a Beethoven symphony, but whatever *agape* is, it was not the friendship Epicurus advocated for normal relations with other human beings.

Friendship is the positive element that makes for a happy person and a successful community. In that way it functions for the Epicurean somewhat as love does for the Christian. On the negative side, the

Epicureans held that bodily pain is to be avoided as far as possible. Pain will of course include violent and threatening discomforts such as starvation, paralysis, nausea, thirst, etc. Sometimes these things cannot be avoided: if they are very severe, they will kill you, and you will never feel suffering again; but if they are moderate, they can be endured. Epicurus himself died in the former way, by all accounts maintaining a quiet acceptance of what was happening. Part of his last letter survives: 'Seven days before writing this, the stoppage [of urine] became complete, and I suffered pains such as bring men to their last day.'

The fear from which we need to be free, according to Epicurus, is not fear of political or military violence. Not a lot can be done about that, except making ourselves inconspicuous; and for the sake of a sustained prospect of a happy life, we should not make our happiness depend upon luxuries that are easily lost or taken away. The freedom that is within our power is freedom from superstitious fears, from fear of gods, and from the fear of death. As we have seen, for Epicurus either there are no gods, or they are unconcerned with us. Hence we are free to search for and to find the causes of natural phenomena, earthquakes, diseases, lightning and everything else without regarding them as god-sent ('Nothing is ever created out of nothing by divine will'), and we are free to make the best we can of the only life we shall ever have. When death comes, it is nothing at all, no more fearful than looking back on the eternity of our non-being before we were born.

The humanity and kindly moderation of so much of what Epicurus had to say is best not summarized but seen in his own sayings. A few will show the man. Don't hurry over them.

No pleasure is in itself evil, but the things that produce certain pleasures result in disturbances many times greater than the pleasures themselves.

You tell me that the stimulus of the flesh makes you too prone to the pleasures of *eros*. Do as you please, provided you do not break the law or defy good customs, and do not distress any of your neighbours, or harm your own body, or impoverish yourself.

Nothing satisfies him for whom enough is too little.

Poverty, when measured by the natural purposes of life,
is great wealth, but unlimited wealth is great poverty.

If you wish to make Pythocles rich, do not give him
more money, but diminish his desires.

Let nothing be done in life that will cause you fear
if it becomes known to your neighbours.

We must laugh and philosophize at the same time,
and do our household duties.

We must free ourselves from the bondage of politics
and public affairs.

Vain is the word of a philosopher that does not heal
the sufferings of man.

Death is nothing to us; for the body, when it has been
resolved into its elements, has no feeling, and that which
has no feeling is nothing to us.

It is not difficult to see that the portrayal of Epicurus' followers – as
self-indulgent pleasure-seekers, satisfied with nothing but a fastidi-
ously selected succession of sensual delights – stands the truth on its
head. Step aside as far as possible from the disturbances of the world,
yes. But then make your happiness depend as little as possible upon the
possession of goods and their continual acquisition. Why? Because
needless wealth leads to restless discontent, and it puts your happiness
upon a footing that can be made precarious by others – a stock market
crash, a war, a credit failure, a fire or a burglary.

So why, unlike the Stoic, is the Epicurean so falsely represented? It
started with the hostility of the Stoics themselves. Both as philosophers and as men of affairs they were concerned with the performance
of public duties and with action. They (particularly the Roman elite)

tended to look unfavourably upon communities like the Epicureans, and later the Christians, who tried to live apart from the state and its obligations. The misrepresentation continued in the 2nd century AD and onwards with the understandable but unrelenting hostility of Christianity.

Epicureanism and Christianity were diametrically opposed at every point in their accounts of the universe, of life and of the afterlife – or lack of it. What was worse, they were not merely philosophically opposed, but were contending for followers in order to establish communities whose living precepts were, remarkable to note, not wildly different. The Epicureans were the losers. The more uncomfortable and precarious this world became, the greater the appeal to the poor, the dispossessed, the sick and the hopeless of a religion that offered eternal bliss in another world, and never mind what happens to you in this – the very proposition that the Epicureans so articulately rejected.

The 'garden in the wilderness' of a meaningless universe, shared with friends who have learnt to enjoy quietness and to find happiness in simple things easily possessed, is an ideal as far from being realized today as the expectations of the Christian communities that replaced them. But in some ways the Epicureans have triumphed without being noticed. Their idea of an infinite universe of matter and space, indifferent to human hopes and concerns, whose workings can be understood without reference to supernatural powers, is the scientific ethos in which we now live. We have fellow feeling with the importance Epicurus attached to happiness in this life, with his desire to diminish pain and to overcome irrational fears, and with his attempt to understand and come to terms with death – the frontier we approach just as he did, but need not reach with fear and trembling if, as Lucretius so powerfully urges, it is the gateway to nothing at all.

The last word

There is a city in south-west Asia Minor you may visit. It is Oinoanda. It is somewhat difficult to reach, tumbled by earthquakes and long abandoned by man. But inscriptions of great value have been found there. There is, for example, a complete and detailed set of regulations granted by Hadrian for the holding of a music festival in the city. It is dated

An ancient Epicurean (at rear) happy with his bread and water. At front, a modern Epicurean!

29 August in the year AD 125. Of roughly the same date, or a bit later, is an inscription originally carved on what was probably a wall of the marketplace. It was in the region of 25,000 words – by far the longest stone inscription ever contrived in Classical (or any other?) times.

This inscription was constructed on the authority and at the expense of a certain Diogenes, who must have been rich, who was by his own admission old and in ill health, who wintered on Rhodes, and who left for posterity – albeit in a shattered state, with many of the stones broken, scattered or lost – the last known Classical exposition of the Epicurean philosophy. About 6,500 words have been recovered, much of it through the exertions of Professor Martin Smith of Durham University.

As with Epicurus, so with Diogenes: it is best to let him speak for himself. Lines near the beginning have achieved a certain fame:

> Having already reached the sunset of my life (being almost
> on the verge of departure from the world on account of age),
> I wanted, before being taken by death, to compose a glad song
> to celebrate the fulness of my happiness, and so to help now
> those who are well-constituted. If one person, or two, or three
> or four, or any large number you choose, provided it is not very
> large, were in a bad predicament … [I would help each as best
> I can]. … But now, as I have said, the most of men lie sick, as it
> were of a pestilence, in their false beliefs about the world, and
> the tale of them increases; for by imitation they take the disease
> from one another, like sheep. And further, it is only just to bring
> help to those who shall come after us – for they too are ours,
> though they be yet unborn; and love for man commands us also
> to help strangers who may pass this way.

And later:

> [We contrived this inscription] … for those who are called
> foreigners, though they are not really so. For while the
> various segments of the earth give different people a different
> country, the whole compass of this world gives all people a
> single country, the entire earth, and a single home, the world.

Diogenes is a little verbose, as some old men (and not a few writers on philosophy) are, but he is also kindly, and conveys a gentle message in the afternoon of a world where the shadows of false belief are already falling. His Epicurean medicine is familiar, but freshly worded:

> One must regard wealth beyond what is natural as of no
> more use than water to a container that is overflowing.

> Public speaking is full of agitation and nervousness as
> to whether one can pull it off.

> We ought to make statues of the gods genial and smiling,
> so that we may smile back at them rather than be afraid.

In his wildest dreams Diogenes of Oinoanda could not have imagined that almost two thousand years later those who are well-constituted would be able to read his words in diverse places throughout his hoped-for single home of the world. But his largest hope is, alas, still our hope:

> We shall not achieve wisdom universally, since not all are
> capable of it. But if we assume it to be possible, then truly
> the life of the gods will pass to men. For everything will
> be full of justice and mutual love, and there will be no need
> of armaments or laws and all the things we contrive on
> account of fear of one another.

* * *

For those who know Greek, the Epicureans are for the most part relatively easy to read in the original. There are dozens of translations of Lucretius. A good one by W. H. D. Rouse and M. Ferguson Smith can be found in the Loeb Classical Library (Cambridge, Mass., 1992). A very tolerable verse translation by R. Melville is in the Oxford World's Classics series (1999). A complete edition of the works of Epicurus and Lucretius is available in one volume: *The Epicurean Philosophers*, edited by John Gaskin (London, 1995). For Diogenes, see *Diogenes of Oinoanda: The Epicurean Inscription* by M. F. Smith (Naples, 1993).

8

Stoicism: Duty and the Laws of Nature

Unlike other schools of philosophy in the ancient world, the Stoics did not perpetuate the name of their founder in their own name. He was Zeno of Citium, in Cyprus, and was born about 335 BC. He came to Athens in 313, and seems to have studied with various Socratic and Platonic philosophers. In due course – the year is not known – he began to teach in his own right, at the *Stoa Poikile*, the 'Painted Colonnade', on one side of the marketplace in Athens. It is from the *stoa* that this most revered of ancient philosophies, later favoured by the elite of the Roman Empire, got its name. Zeno died in 263 BC.

Zeno created a system of thought developed, like that of Epicurus, in three stages: a logic that included an account of language and a theory of knowledge; a physics with a cosmology awesome enough to stand comparison with that of recent years; and an ethic, a way of responding to our place in the physical vastness of the universe that has never wholly perished from the earth.

Hard hills and lost maps

It is possible to give some account of Stoicism to anyone who is willing to think, but to do justice to the way in which it was developed and defended by Zeno's successors eludes even the finest scholars. There are three reasons for this. The first is that the system is complex. It used difficult ideas, some of them contrary to common sense. It tried to be comprehensive in the grandest way, and it defended itself over long periods of time with a variety of arguments of great ingenuity.

The second reason is that Stoicism was an evolving, not a static, system. In the two centuries after Zeno's death, a progression of distinguished advocates and opponents – names that would now fall upon deaf ears at even the most sophisticated of cocktail parties – argued the system's merits, adapting and correcting it in the process, somewhat akin to the way a scientific theory is refined by peer review.

The third reason why Stoicism is so difficult to grasp fully – and it is the greatest intellectual disaster of the Classical world – is that the prolific writings of these same academic Stoics in the period of its Hellenistic development are entirely lost. Of Zeno, Chrysippus, Panaetius and Posidonius, to name but a few, all we have are brief quotations, references, summaries, and the employment of the system as a life-guide by later Roman writers whose works have survived.

The first of these was Cicero (106–43 BC). Although not entirely in favour of what his Stoic teachers were saying, in his late writings on Greek philosophy for Roman readers he brings us as close to men like Posidonius as we can get. Seneca (*c.* 4 BC–AD 65) was the able administrator of the Roman Empire under the first eight (sane!) years of Nero's rule. His *Moral Essays* (sometimes called *Dialogues on Morality*) and *Epistles* (also known as the *Letters to Lucilius*) – not to mention his hilarious skit on the experiences of the late Emperor Claudius in an afterlife – make good reading. The third of the Roman writers, Epictetus (*c.* AD 50– *c.* 120), is more demanding reading. The last is Marcus Aurelius (121–180 AD), Roman emperor from 161–180 AD, whose private notes and moral reflections (much humbler than those of the ex-slave), known as the *Meditations*, have survived by some joyous chance of history.

So what of this great and enduring system? As with the Epicureans, I must exclude the logic. It was good stuff, and represents the only significant development in the field between Aristotle and George Boole in the 19th century, but it demands philosophical archaeology and technical fuss that most of us would not welcome. The physics is truly exciting but requires imagination and attention. The ethics are easily understandable, though closely enmeshed with the physics.

The intelligible universe

Because so much of the source material is lost, we cannot properly reconstruct the reasons the Stoics had for the first principles of their physics, but in outline the picture is this:

❖ The universe, the ALL, is infinite void, plus a vast but finite continuum of matter that makes up the cosmos or ORDERED whole. (Note the difference from the Epicureans, for whom the universe is infinite matter moving randomly in infinite space.)

❖ Matter – whatever is in the void – is an inert stuff. It is infused with an intelligible activity that the Stoics identified as an indwelling fiery air, or *pneuma*. (Note again the contrast with the Epicureans, for whom the stuff – the primary particles – and the movement of the particles are not separable. Particles and their random movement are a single given fact of nature.) For us, the Stoic contrast between 'stuff' and *pneuma* might be made a little clearer if we think of their stuff as the wire, and their *pneuma* as the electricity within it.

❖ The *pneuma* shows itself as pattern, order, the intelligibility of the cosmos; it is whatever it is we can discern as the laws of nature – the *logos* or reason of things. This 'reason of things' the Stoics often, and confusingly, called God – not the personal agent with semi-human concerns we are all familiar with now, but the ordered, cosmic, understandable workings of nature.

The laws of nature

Within the *logos* of nature, the Stoics identified three very general or over-arching principles of natural law. These principles – which are capable of generating, and have indeed generated, a vast array of particular scientific laws and theories – are: causal determinism; gravity or *hexis*; and the idea of an expanding dynamic universe.

1 **Causal determinism.** Cicero vividly articulates this principle in his *Of Divination*, where he may well be paraphrasing or quoting his teacher Posidonius:

> By fate I mean … an orderly succession of causes wherein cause is linked to cause, and each cause of itself produces an effect … Therefore nothing has happened which was not bound to happen, and likewise nothing is going to happen which will not find in nature every efficient cause of its happening. Consequently fate is called, not ignorantly, but as a physical principle 'the eternal cause of things, the wherefore of things past, of things present, and of things to come' … For he who knows the causes of future events

necessarily knows what every future event will be …
Things which are to be do not suddenly spring into
existence, but the evolution of time is like the unwinding
of a rope bringing forth nothing new, but only unfolding
each event in its order.

The challenge to look for particular causal chains – a basic
activity of science – is manifest. Almost as clear are the somewhat
disturbing apparently deterministic consequences for human
freedom of action and responsibility – a problem the Stoics
struggled over with only moderate success.

2 **Gravity or** *hexis*. The Stoics presumed the existence of a force
that must operate in order to stop individual things, and the great
cosmos itself, from coming apart and ultimately dispersing into
the infinite void of the universe. On a more local scale it could,
they thought, explain the tidal motions of the ocean 'in sympathy
with the moon'.

3 **The expanding cosmos.** The Stoics regarded the behaviour of the
cosmos as cyclical, and in its present state it is moving outwards.
At the beginning of this process, a process in which we now exist,
a fireball of matter infused with the *pneuma* bursts out and
becomes the cosmos – an expanding, dynamic system. The
expanding forces will eventually give way to the *hexis* of
attracting forces, and all will collapse back into destruction. It
will then burst out anew in a pulsating cosmos. This is a fanciful
notion, but perhaps not quite as fanciful as it seemed a few
decades ago, given the prevailing scientific theory that
everything started with the Big Bang. Seneca puts the idea across
vividly in his essay *To Marcia, on Consolation*:

> And when the time shall come for the world to be blotted out
> in order that it may begin its life anew, these things will destroy
> themselves by their own power, and stars will clash with stars,
> and all the fiery matter of the world that now shines in orderly
> array will blaze up in a common conflagration … Then we too,

amid the falling universe, shall be added as a tiny fraction to this mighty destruction ... when it shall seem best to god to create the universe anew.

The bridge of nature

I now come to one of the most inspired and extraordinary ideas ever propounded. It may not be credible. It may not even make sense; but at least it has the power to make us think – and wonder.

The connection that the Stoics proposed between ourselves and the cosmos as a whole is that we are a part of the continuum of the cosmos both as inert stuff and as active intelligence or reason. To put it in words never (as far as I know) actually used by the Hellenistic Stoics: intelligence – that with which we *act* – and the intelligibility or reason of things in the cosmos – its order, regularity, lawfulness, or 'god' – are different aspects of the same thing. We are a tiny part of the reason of things that acts. We are also part of the stuff of the cosmos and subject to its laws. Within us we have the free, active fire that is our own will, but as stuff we have very great limitations. None of us can live for ever. Few of us could have written Haydn's quartets, or walked unscathed through a burning fiery furnace. Many of us could not run a mile in under four minutes. But we can accept our limitations and achieve within our abilities.

The problem of reconciling our freedom and responsibility with the existence of necessitating causes worried the Stoics just as it has, in different ways, also worried us. Chrysippus' solution – or at least the way he tried to get rid of the problem – seems to have been to argue that our assent to what happens to us is not necessitated. Although it has some external necessitating causes – our genetic make-up and the conditions of our upbringing, for instance – our assent itself, our attitude to what happens, derives at least in part from something internal to us, which is our freedom. This something is our reason. Aristotle, with his usual incisive good sense, comes close to Chrysippus' solution: 'There is a stage in the development of our characters, before our disposition becomes hardened into determining habits, when we can turn another way, and in that sense we are responsible for what we are and do.'

These arguments touch upon some of the most complex and disputed areas of philosophy. The Greeks could afford to argue; the Romans wanted a usable product that would give them a sense of responsibility for the men who were under their command and the empire that was under their protection. Their working solution can be gleaned from Cicero's short essay *On Fate*. He may be quoting one of the earlier Hellenistic Stoics when he says:

> Although we admit that it does not rest with ourselves whether we are quick-witted or dull, strong or weak, yet the person who thinks that it necessarily follows from this that even our choice between sitting still and walking about is not within our power fails to discern the true sequence of cause and effect. For, granted that clever people and stupid people are born like that, owing to antecedent causes, and that the same is true of the strong and the weak, nevertheless it does not follow that our sitting and walking and performing any act are also defined and constituted by primary causes … [Consider Socrates, whose character was read by a physiognomist as that of a thick-witted womanizer.] It is possible these defects may be due to natural causes; but their eradication and entire removal, recalling the man himself from the serious vices to which he was inclined, does not rest with natural causes, but with will, effort and training.

Our physical structure and character traits are thus predetermined, but we have the freedom to make the best of them. We are not entirely slaves to our characters. In particular we control our responses by thought – that is our freedom, our part of the active fire, the reason of things. We can go kicking and screaming into the dark night; or we can go with dignity, perhaps at a time of our own choosing, knowing that we have willed in accordance with the order of things, and accepted what must be. (The Stoics had no problems with a rational decision to kill oneself.)

Personal integrity and suffering

There is one principle of Stoicism that, unless explained, sounds very odd. It is that pain is not an evil, nor pleasure a good. This is because, for the Stoics, 'evil' and 'good' refer only to one's internal state of mind, not to external things that affect us. Health, good food and a sufficiency of worldly goods are 'appropriate' for us as human beings, but not necessary to our internal integrity. Similarly, sickness, pain and poverty are 'inappropriate', but need not destroy the inner person. There is even a sense in which physical hardship can improve the inner person. Thus Seneca writes, in his essay *On Providence*:

> I may say to a good man, 'You are unfortunate because you have never been unfortunate; you have passed through life without an antagonist. No one will know what you can do – not even you yourself. For if a man is to know himself, he must be tried.

Nevertheless, it has to be admitted that, for all the moral and philosophical nobility of Stoicism, in the their pursuit of strict rational consistency the academic Stoics were capable of following their principles into conclusions contrary to all common sense. Cicero and Plutarch (AD 46–*c.* 120) both wrote critiques of Stoic absurdities, and their criticisms are those of wise men of the world. But the grand outlines of the system remained intact for the individual human being to work with in their lives. Of these individuals, and there were (and are) many, one stands above all others.

Marcus Aurelius

No one ever tried to put into practice the principles of Stoicism from a more exalted position or with a stronger sense of duty than the Roman emperor Marcus Aurelius Antoninus. His private *Meditations* is an extraordinary document, consisting of paragraphs and sentences written at odd moments in a desperately hard working life as a reflection upon what he tried to do and to be. Don't read it like a book. Open it at random in a few places. You will find the silly, the trivial, the complex, the superstitious, the commonplace – and some of the profoundest thoughts a human being can have about his place in the great company of the world. Let a few samples speak for themselves:

> Keep yourself a simple and a good man, uncorrupt, dignified, plain, a friend of justice, god-fearing, gracious, affectionate, manful in doing your duty ... Revere the gods, serve mankind. Life is short.

> At daybreak, when reluctant to get up, have this thought ready to mind: 'I am rising for a man's work.' Am I then still peevish

that I am going to do that for which I was born, and for the
sake of which I came into the world? Or was I made for this,
that I should nuzzle under the bedclothes and keep warm?
But this is pleasanter! Have you then been made for pleasure?
In a word, I ask you, to be acted upon [by circumstances] or
to take action?

Men cannot praise you for sharpness of wit. But there are
other qualities of which you can say 'I had that by nature.' Well
then, display those which are in your power! [The emperor is
addressing himself.]

Do not feel sickness or despondency or discomfort if you do
not always succeed in acting from right principles. When you
are defeated, return again to them, and rejoice if on the whole
your conduct is worthy of a man, and love the course to which
you have returned.

If someone hurts you, reflect that they are akin to you, and
do wrong through ignorance, and that within a short time
both you and they will be gone; and above all that the man
has not really harmed you, for he has not made the ruling
reason within you worse than it was before.

An angry scowl on the face is beyond measure unnatural,
and when often there, all comeliness begins to die away and
in the end can never be rekindled.

Few, if any, world rulers have a reputation as high as that of Marcus
Aurelius. Matthew Arnold justly described him as 'one of the best of
men'. But there is a weariness about his nobility. He was a lover of
peace, but almost his entire reign was taken up with wars, in the north
and east, to defend the empire, and nothing says this with more sad
acceptance than his own words in *Meditations* II.17:

Life is a warfare and a pilgrim's sojourn, and fame after death
is only forgetfulness … But if there be nothing terrible in each

thing being continually changed into another, why should a
man look askance at the change and dissolution of all things?
For it is in the way of nature, and in nature there can be no evil.

Finally:

Human beings have been created for the sake of one another.
Therefore either assist or endure.

Although he was quite critical of the Stoics, no one ever put
Marcus Aurelius' last point better than Cicero, in sentences that were
to open the way for what would become the theory of natural law as it
relates to human society. In *De legibus* ('On the laws'), he writes: 'No
single thing is so like another thing as all of us are like each other'; and
in *De finibus* ('On ends'): 'The mere fact of their common humanity
requires that one man should find another to be akin to him.' Cicero
and the emperor are beginning to express the wonderful idea of the
brotherhood of man: that at some level we are all the same, with the
same needs, hopes and obligations to one another. Yet Cicero goes
further, in a famous passage from his *Republic*, invoking the idea of a
universal law applicable to all humanity:

True law is right reason in agreement with nature; it is
of universal application, unchanging and everlasting …
We cannot be freed from its obligations by senate or people,
and we need not look outside ourselves for an expounder
or interpreter of it. And there will not be different laws at
Rome and at Athens, or different laws now and in the future,
but one eternal and unchangeable law will be valid for all
men and all times, and there will be one master and ruler,
god, over us all, for he is the author of this law. (III.22)

If we interpret Cicero's god as the Stoics' 'reason of things', this is a statement about the order of the cosmos as it might apply to human society:
we are all part of one grand system, as Marcus Aurelius tried to be.

On grounds well thought out by the Greeks and accepted by the
Romans, Stoicism thus offers as a way of life:

Marcus Aurelius curled up in bed. (Note the warm cat under his feet.)

❖ An assurance that the individual is part of a whole that has *some* meaning.

❖ A way of enduring misfortune and disappointment by the strength of one's inward integrity.

❖ A way of warning ourselves that we should not value too much our own achievements; they are at best little and soon forgotten.

❖ A way of commending the human will as captain of one's soul, despite its being bound by the necessities of the laws of nature.

❖ A way of connecting us with the lives of others as part of the system of human society, and in the end of accepting death as natural and inevitable, and as a returning to the peace that was ours before we were born. As the English poet John Drinkwater was to put it two thousand years later, 'Nor ... is the doom anything / Memorable for its apparelling; / The bearing of man facing it is all.'

Stoicism never entirely perished from the earth, but after about AD 200 it slowly gave way to extravagantly mystical philosophies and new religions. Why? Because Stoicism as a way of life was for the strong-minded, the thoughtful, the vigorous and the powerful. Christianity offered everything to the weak and the dispossessed, and demanded not thought and complex argument, but faith; and faith, once granted, can move mountains. Thought is always hard, and in the end may have to acknowledge that mountains stay where they are.

* * *

A good general account of Stoicism can be found in A. A. Long's *Hellenistic Philosophy* (London, 1974; revd edn 1986), and a more complete account of their physics in *Physics of the Stoics* by S. Sambursky (London, 1959). Dip into any paragraph of the *Meditations* to go further with the thoughts of Marcus Aurelius. There are scores of translations. Seneca's 124 *Letters* are short and very readable; a translation is available in the Penguin Classics (Harmondsworth, 1974). His *Moral Essays* are splendidly translated by J. W. Basore in three much-reprinted volumes of the Loeb Classical Library (Cambridge, Mass., 1928–35).

9

Neoplatonism:
The Last Protest

The progress – that is probably still the right word – of philosophy and science after the rule of the first Roman emperor, Caesar Augustus (r. 31 BC–AD 14), is not just the self-absorbed twittering of an intellectual elite. Philosophical teaching continued to be widely accessible. Brilliant scientific work was done by, among others, Galen of Pergamon (AD 129–?199/216), in medicine and anatomy; and in astronomy by Ptolemy of Alexandria (*fl.* AD 146–170).

The famous schools of philosophy in Athens (Plato's Academy, Aristotle's Lyceum, the Stoa and the Epicurean Garden) continued in various manifestations, and indeed were all provided with funds from the imperial treasury by Marcus Aurelius. But the creative excitement of free debate concerning nature, the cosmos and human society that had characterized thought from the Milesians to the Stoics and Epicurus faded into a period of maintenance, annotation, and the eclectic gathering of ideas to make superficially attractive omelettes from incompatible eggs. There was, moreover, a new force in the world that would change everything.

No exact date can be put upon such things, but after the death of Marcus Aurelius in AD 180, new religions and quasi-religions – most conspicuously Christianity and Gnosticism – exerted a slowly increasing pressure upon philosophical thought. The theologians (a new concept in human expertise) set about defining their beliefs and disputing with one another, using arguments developed by the philosophers for other purposes. You can still see one such example in the Nicene Creed, used during the Eucharist, which describes Christ as 'being of one substance with the Father': 'substance' is a concept borrowed from Aristotle. By the end of the 4th century only those techniques of philosophy that were actively helpful to religion were cherished. Those viewed as neutral or indifferent were preserved out of scholarly interest, if at all; those that were hostile, for example the works of Epicurus and Porphyry, were actively destroyed; and the Classical world ended in a flurry of barbarian conquests in the West, and in other worldly mysticism and new religions in the East.

The last non-Christian emperor, Julianus Augustus (Julian the Apostate), died in AD 363, and with him went the last hope for any long-term coexistence between religion and secular philosophy. In the West, Rome was sacked by the Visigoths in 410, by the Vandals in 451, and the last Western emperor was deposed in 476. In the East, at Constantinople, the empire continued triumphantly, but in a system that, in ideological terms, can only be described as theological totalitarianism. It was a small thing in itself, but the final crushing blow against the old ways of thinking came in 527, with the closure of the surviving non-Christian schools in Athens by order of Justinian, and the dispersal to the East of their last professors.

Yet there had been one last flowering of Classical philosophy in the 3rd century AD, albeit a system of extravagantly rationalized mysticism. It was the philosophy of Plotinus (AD 204–270), which much later became known as Neoplatonism. What makes it a philosophy rather than a religion is that it is argued, not asserted from some dogmatic revelation, and never presented as the rationalization of some previously accepted belief. In that way it is still in the Socratic tradition of 'following the argument wherever it leads' – even if it leads to a sustained effort to say the unsayable and think the unthinkable.

Plotinus

The first certain fact about Plotinus is that he went to Alexandria when he was aged 27 to study philosophy, and that he stayed there until AD 243, when he migrated to Rome and himself began to teach what he regarded as the real meaning of Plato's work. He wrote nothing until he was about 50 years old, meaning that in a modern university he would either have been forced into early retirement or have become a vice-chancellor. His works – fifty-four essays arguing his version of Platonism – were edited, presented and published by his biographer and student Porphyry in about 300, and they survived to convey the ideas of a semi-mystical Platonism to later European philosophy.

Both Plotinus and Porphyry (himself a major philosopher) rejected Christianity because of its reliance on faith rather than on reason, and because its supernaturalism was based upon a person and addressed to individuals. There was, however, an ambivalence in the relationship between Plotinus' Platonism and the religion whose definition of orthodoxy was being argued, and sometimes fought over, in Constantinople. Porphyry's book *Against the Christians* was burnt, and no copy survives. The last philosophers expelled from Athens in 529 were Neoplatonists. But Neoplatonist schools were widespread in the 4th century AD, and large elements of their teaching were incorporated into Christian philosophy and theology until as recently as the Cambridge Platonists in the 17th century, the English poet William Blake, and the French philosopher Henri Bergson, who died in 1941.

Neoplatonism: The 'great chain of being'

The emphasis of so much Greek philosophy on self-control and moderation, and its tendency to downgrade riches and celebrity – in Epicurus' aphorism, 'If you wish to make Pythocles rich, do not give him more money, but diminish his desires' – would never have commended itself to the television personality, the investment banker or the professional sportsman struggling to make ends meet on a few million a year. But Plotinus' philosophy is unfashionable in another way. It is alarmingly metaphysical and far from the world of our ordinary understanding. The trouble is that, read into deeply, it is also strangely convincing. Alas, all I can offer here is an unappetizing glimpse of a meal that may be worth eating.

As I tried to explain in Chapter 5, one element of Plato's philosophy can be described as a two-world theory of reality. There is a 'this world' of ordinary fallible perception, and another world of immaterial souls, permanent realities and intelligible forms. Plotinus thought this dualism a mistaken understanding of Plato. He did not seek to refute it with the hard-headed rationalism and worldly good sense of Aristotle, nor with the comprehensive one-world universe of the Epicureans or Stoics. Instead, he created a vast unitary system of reality in which all that is, exists in ultimate dependence upon a reality that is the ONE – incorporeal, self-caused, absolutely free and good. The ONE is being without beginning or end, from which all else emanates in a descending series of lesser realities, each one of which is more fragmented, numerous and separated from the ONE than the previous.

The first stage below absolute being – the ONE – is World–Mind, *Nous* or Intellect, which emanates from the superabundant reservoir of existence and life like light from an inexhaustible sun. Plotinus calls it 'vision that has not yet achieved sight', becoming 'many' as distinct from the ONE.

The second stage of this projection is World–Soul, or *Psuche*: an emanation from *Nous*. The World–Soul is the universal principle of life, including within itself all individual souls.

The third and lowest stage of dependence on the ONE is an emanation of *Psuche*. It is the material universe of space–time. All bodily forms are contained within the boundless ocean of World–Soul.

Below that comes formless matter: the passive stuff of sensible things, so remote from the ONE that, by contrast, it must be called evil.

Yes, I know: you are lost, like so many wonderers before you. But through the rationalized mysticism of his vast system, Plotinus, with the help of Porphyry, carried a version of Plato's ideas through the Dark Ages and into medieval Europe. His works, alone with those of Plato, survived entire from the wreckage of antiquity. If his own writings are acutely difficult and demanding, Porphyry's *Life*, written as a preface to his gathering of Plotinus' works for publication, is easy. Let Porphyry have the last word; or, rather, let Homer have the very last word, at the closing of Classical antiquity, as he had at the beginning:

> When Plotinus had written anything, he could never bear
> to go over it twice; even to read it through once was too
> much for him as his eyesight was poor. In writing he did
> not form the letters with any regard to appearance or
> divide his syllables correctly, and he paid no attention to
> spelling. He was wholly concerned with thought; and, which
> surprised us all, he went on in this way right up to the end.
> He worked out his train of thought from beginning to end
> in his own mind ... and wrote as continuously as if he were
> copying from a book ... He generally expressed himself in
> a tone of rapt inspiration ... 'a light to men'.

10

The End of Classical Antiquity

No single thing abides; but all things flow.
Fragment to fragment clings – the things thus grow
Until we know and name them. By degrees
They melt, and are no more the things we know.

So Lucretius, writing about the nature of the universe at large; but he
could equally have been writing about the speed of change in human
lives and institutions. If we compare the world of Alexander and
Aristotle, in about 325 BC, with the world of Hadrian and Galen in the
2nd century AD, much has changed, but much is still recognizable: the
world is bigger, more complicated, embraces more people and cultures;
there are more divinities to choose from. Within its wider frontiers it is
safer, richer, on the way to being more cruel, but still open to speculation and freedom of thought in a way that Classical Hellenism would
recognize. Religions, buildings, civic life, temples and their functions,
theatres and their activities, schools and public games all show a continuity. Literacy, especially in the East, is relatively common, and books
and papyrus rolls are preserved and respected. In philosophy and
science it is still possible to 'follow wherever the argument leads'.

Yet if we compare this world with the world of the early 5th
century AD – the world that followed the death of the Eastern Roman
emperor Theodosius in 395, and in which Augustine had converted to
Christianity – all is social and intellectual change in the East, and
destruction in the West. The destruction is military, ethnic and political; it can be followed in the vividly documented narrative of J. B.
Ward-Perkins's aptly named book *The Fall of Rome and the End of
Civilization* (Oxford, 2005). The change in the East, on the other hand,
is religious, cultural and philosophical. It has the effect of altering or
abandoning almost everything that would be recognizable to Classical
Hellenism or that might have been approved by Hadrian. The very

structure of cities changes, leaving – where the sites decayed or were abandoned – the mighty ruins of the previous age that we see today.

What produced this shattering of the traditional world, which no war or decisive invasion caused? There is one answer whose apparent simplicity hides so much: religion.

Leaving aside the conflicting possibilities of divine intention favouring St Paul, why did Classical paganism and all the antique freedoms that went with it fail, and Christianity with all its apparent weakness succeed? The question is too profound to be answered briefly; too interesting and germane to what one sees on the ground to be entirely ignored.

Paganism

The tolerant confusion that was Classical paganism is best described in negatives – by setting out which aspects familiar to modern monotheistic religion it lacked. (This lack, incidentally, facilitated scientific and philosophical ideas in a way that Christianity did not, and in some manifestations – concerning evolution, for instance – still does not.)

1 Pagan deities are not subject to death like us, and in that sense they are the immortals, yet they are a part of the universe – an awesome, immensely powerful, invisible part, of which it behoves us to be aware, but a part all the same. They are not the creators and sustainers of all that is, and not the distant and final reason why everything is as it is.

2 The deities are not exclusive. No human and no god would be justifiably offended if you worshipped Athene at Athens, Artemis at Ephesus, and were also a member of a Mithraic lodge on the north British frontier (hence the saying, 'When in Rome, do as the Romans do'). In his account of piety, Socrates offers a more philosophically interesting interpretation of the same idea: piety is 'the art that gods and men have of trafficking with one another' – a sort of divine–human constitutional arrangement.

3 Given the free-for-all nature of the ancient gods, in which cults and new divinities come and sometimes go, it should be unsurprising

to note that there are no creeds, no systematic theologies, no national or internationally organized priesthood, no book with divine authority whose interpretation must be precisely settled and, if necessary, fought over, and hence there is no heresy.

4 To follow pagan religion is to avoid giving offence by unseemly behaviour within a place in which the god took most delight – the sanctuary, the sacred grove, or any area marked out for the gods. The god must be pleasured with the smoke of sacrifice, and with plays or hymns correctly spoken and ceremonies correctly performed. This applies also to the countless minor divinities of hearth, forest, field and waters, who expected much lesser observances. The result is a kind of compact or bargain between men and gods: we do our best to observe you, and you help us if it pleases you.

5 The idea of sin – separation from the grace of a deity by knowing disregard of his or her will – scarcely exists in Classical polytheism. You may fail to perform a ceremony correctly by carelessness or accident; you may omit some local observance and thus locally offend some god who may harm you; you may even, like Orestes, break some absolute *praxis* or code of behaviour and be punished until the god changes the rules – but you may think what you like. You cannot commit a sin inside your own head through disbelief or desire for the forbidden, or through any speculation or belief about the nature of the universe.

6 Finally, good relations between ourselves and a god or gods in this life give no promise of either eternal bliss or eternal punishment.

So, in sum, unlike Christian or Islamic monotheism, Classical polytheism saw its divinities as beings who:

❖ were a part of the universe

❖ did not grant everlasting life in exchange for belief in them

❖ made no claim to exclude other divinities, who in any case were often their relatives or themselves under other names (there was, therefore, no problem of religious toleration)

❖ embodied a religion that required no national or international uniformity and had no sacred text with divine authority – hence there was no general concept of orthodoxy or heresy

❖ had no absolute evil being – no Satan – in their pantheon

How this religious climate, so utterly different from the one that succeeded it, made easier the beginnings of science and philosophy can be readily understood. But think just for a moment of the religious opposition to Galileo in the 17th century, or the creationists' continuing objections to the theory of evolution. Had these theories been developed in Classical antiquity – and, in fact, both were – no one would have used piety to the gods as an objection to them. The gods as worshipped were not responsible for the general nature of the universe.

The new way
Why did this religiously tolerant, untidy Classical world give way, in the end so speedily, to a religion that excluded all others? To a religion that was organized in the Eastern Roman Empire from the beginning, and among the ruins of the Western Empire after slow and painful effort, as a theocratic state? A general answer is that the Christian convert had a totally different outlook on life, death and suffering from his or her pagan counterpart and predecessors, and they had faith. In brief:

1 The Christian had extraordinary strength. He or she believed absolutely and without reservation that the truth they possessed would give them everlasting life whatever happened to them in this life, be it suffering, poverty, social deprivation or horrible death. Suffering now does not matter: it is the precursor to the heavenly bliss that will follow the resurrection of the dead at the Second Coming.

2 Christianity was open to all, however wretched, ill-connected, illiterate or deprived. It was the religion for the outsider, the underdog – those for whom the great empire of the world offered little but servitude and non-entity, and it offered forgiveness for those who felt sinful.

3 Collision with the Roman state was inevitable, and eventually looked for. The early Christian communities – like the Epicureans, only much more obviously – tended to form a state within a state that refused to play the game. But the Epicureans had no more qualms about offering the expected worship at the shrine of a deified emperor than at the shrine of any other god. Belief was not an issue. The Christian, however, could not do this. There was only one God; all others were devils or fictions. This civic or imperial non-participation, or active disobedience, was the source of the occasional, erratic and for much of the time local persecution of Christian communities, not their beliefs as such. By the time any consistent persecution of the Christians was attempted, it was too little and too late. Why? Because, according to the bishops, martyrdom would result in immediate reception into the arms of God without waiting. The martyrdom was cruel and vile, particularly in North Africa and the Western Empire, but the dreadful thing was that it was wanted, and the Roman state could no more deal with people who wanted to suffer than the modern democratic state can cope with people it calls terrorists but who regard themselves as martyrs destined to everlasting bliss.

4 The early Christian attitude to death and suffering stood the Classical view of these things on its head. The Classical view, going back to Homer, was that death was to be avoided, that there was nothing good about it from the prospect of a living man, and that suffering was undesirable. If it was unrelenting (such as the plague that hit Athens, related by Thucydides), suffering could become an argument against your reliance on the god. The Christians reversed this thinking. The more you suffered, the more you were like the founder of your faith; and the way to everlasting life was through suffering even unto death. Against

that single, unbreakable faith, so appealing to those who had few joys of this world to loose, the power of the Roman state was ultimately helpless.

The final accommodation of Christianity with the state came in two stages: Constantine accepted it for the sake of the unity of the state; Theodosius imposed it without any other permitted option.

The stages of intolerance

The difference – the huge and ultimately all-encompassing difference – between the religion St Paul constructed out of what he had heard about the life of Jesus, and all other sects, cults and forms of worship of the Classical era (leaving aside only the Jews, but they kept themselves to themselves) was that the religion of Paul claimed uniqueness and universality of a sort that precluded, and soon made sinful, all and any other religious belief or observance a human being might have or undertake. Once the religion had acquired power, the outcome was as logical as an Aristotelian syllogism. Politically, the outcome developed under three emperors.

In the famous and admirable Edict of Milan (also known as the Edict of Toleration), issued in AD 313, Constantine decreed:

> We resolved on adopting this policy, namely that we should consider that no one whatsoever should be denied freedom to devote himself either to the cult of the Christians or to such religion as he deems best suited to himself, so that the highest divinity, to whose worship we pay allegiance with free minds, may grant us in all things his wanted favour and benevolence.

Forty-seven years later, having been forced to be a Christian and now emperor in Constantinople, Julianus made almost the last attempt to allow the new and old religions to coexist. In the words of his friend and contemporary Ammianus Marcellinus (c. AD 325–c. 395):

> When his fears were ended [of professing gods], and he saw that the time had come when he could do as he wished, he revealed the secrets of his heart and by plain and formal

decrees ordered the temples to be opened and [sacrifice
and worship of gods] to be restored. And in order to add
to the effectiveness of these ordinances, he summoned to the
palace the bishops of the Christians, who were of conflicting
opinions, and the people who were also at variance, and
politely advised them to lay aside their differences, and each
fearlessly and without opposition to observe his own beliefs …
knowing as he did from experience that no wild beasts are
such enemies to mankind as are most of the Christians in
their deadly hatred of one another. (*History*, XXII.5)

But Julianus was soon dead, having lost his life defending the empire
against the Persians. By the end of the century Theodosius had decided
against the toleration of both paganism and any deviation from what
was being defined as orthodox Christianity. Indeed, his attitude to
other Christians, set out in 381 AD, is a vivid, if unintended, vindication
of Julianus' terrible charge:

The observation of the Nicene faith, handed down from our
ancestors and affirmed by the testimony and declaration of
the divine religion, destined to be continued for ever, will be
maintained. The contamination of the Photinian error, the
poison of the Arian sacrilege, the crime of the Eunomian
heresy, and the unspeakable prodigies of the sects will be
banished from hearing.

And so it continued for hundreds of years. The freedoms of the Classical
world, together with its follies, were gone.

The philosophical change

There is no need to describe and to analyse the change in the use of
reasoning that took place between the departed Hellenic world and the
coming medieval. It can be shown in the constrasting words of two
men, each of the highest possible ability and fame, one from the high
noon of antiquity, the other at its end.

The first is Aristotle. In the much-quoted beginning of the
Metaphysics, he proclaims that 'All men by nature desire knowledge.'

Later in the same work he writes of its accumulation:

> While no one is able to attain the truth adequately …
> everyone says something true about the nature of things, and
> while individually they contribute little or nothing to the
> truth, by the union of all a considerable amount is amassed.

Thus spoke the scientist gathering information, or the research group with a project. Here is Aristotle again, this time in the *Physics*, on how to disagree, and on what is required for a true conclusion:

> It is not enough for anyone [in this context Anaxagoras] to assert
> that this particular succession actually takes place unless he can
> point out its determining principle: he must not lay down or claim
> as an axiom a groundless assumption; on the contrary he must
> produce some inductive or deductive proof of his assertion.

The second man is St Augustine (354–430), writing in his *Confessions* on knowledge about the nature of things. The contrast with Aristotle's delight in finding out about the world is remarkable:

> There is another form of temptation, even more fraught with
> danger. This is the disease of curiosity … It is this which
> drives us to try to discover the secrets of nature, those secrets
> which are beyond our understanding, which can avail us
> nothing, and which man should not wish to learn.

And on how to dispose of opposition:

> What then does brotherly love do? Does it, because it fears
> short-lived furnaces for a few, abandon all to the eternal fires
> of Hell? And does it leave so many to perish everlastingly,
> those whom heretics will not permit to live in accordance
> with the teachings of Christ?

Whatever one's beliefs, it is surely beyond reasonable doubt that the great philosophical systems that could follow wherever the argument led, and that opened the gates of the natural universe, would not have prospered if the systematic development of an omniscient religion had come at the beginning of Classical antiquity rather than at its end. Homer and the Classical world gave birth to what we think; St Paul and Muhammad gave birth to what we believe. The union – or disunion – of the two is where we are now.

* * *

The transformation of the still-Classical world presided over by the emperor Hadrian in the 2nd century AD into the religion-dominated world of the 4th to 5th centuries AD is a fascinating story. By far the best source of evidence and historical sequence is Robin Lane Fox's *Pagans and Christians* (London, 1986; revd edn Harmondsworth, 1988). The emperor Julianus Augustus (Julian the Apostate in Christian demonology) – a subject of endless fascination to European writers and intellectuals – is well served by a recent biography by Adrian Murdoch, *The Last Pagan* (Stroud, 2003). The emperor's own extant works are available in the Loeb Classical Library (3 vols; Cambridge, Mass., 1913–23); try his 'Against the Galileans': it was dictated in a hurry, and much of it was destroyed or damaged by his opponents, but it is still interesting as a 'last protest'. An account of how his world finally changed to one of Byzantine Christianity is vividly given in *AD 381: Heretics, Pagans and the Christian State* (London, 2008), by Charles Freeman. Don't forget Gibbon: his *The Decline and Fall of the Roman Empire* is still one of the finest reads in the English language. Its first three chapters are a splendid account of the empire at its apogee, in the 2nd century AD, while chapters 15 and 16 break new ground. History is written by the victors and, for all their suffering, real and alleged, in the 4th century, the Christians were the victors. In these chapters, Gibbon is the first scholar in fourteen hundred years to re-examine the extent and character of the persecution of Christians, and to find it not quite all that Christian apologists and Hollywood producers tend to assume.

Neoplatonism is terribly difficult to read about. Try the well-established account in Richard T. Wallis's *Neoplatonism* (London, 2nd edn 1995). Porphyry's *Life of Plotinus* can be found in vol. I of the Loeb Classical Library's edition of *Plotinus* (Cambridge, Mass., 1966).

PART III

Cities and Citizens: A Gazetteer

O little city, walled against no foe,
         Why are you here?
         What happened at your end?
High on a hill alone you lie at peace
Beneath the ancient shade of Lycian pines,
With tumbled stadium of matted stones,
And changeless marketplace forever still.
     There is no temple to a careless god,
         No pious rubble of a ruined apse
     To threaten with a needless life to come;
     No mark of cruel sports upon the stage
Where men might with Menander laugh again.
They built and bathed here, talked, and sat beside
The fountains in a place they felt secure.
     O little city broken by the years,
Where shall we build? What happens at our end?
                                        JG

Abdera

Abdera is in Thrace, on the north coast of the Aegean, about 100 km (65 miles) west of the Greek border with Turkey. The nearest substantial modern port is Kavala.

Sadly, there is now little to see on the surface, although Abdera was once an important and extensive city. The archaeologists are slowly rolling back the detritus of two thousand years to expose the outlines of roads and buildings, so the revealed picture will become steadily more interesting. There is an outstandingly well-presented small museum close by at Avdira, where the exhibits found at Abdera are presented according to subject and labelled in English.

Ancient Abdera was founded from the city of Clazomenae (near Bodrum) in about 650 BC, and greatly augmented by the population of Teos (near Ephesus), who fled the Persians in 544 BC, probably bringing with them the poet Anacreon. The city was famous for the quality of its coinage, and prospered on account of its good agricultural land and as a trade route into the hinterland. But despite Cicero twice using the word 'Abderan' to mean 'silly' in his letters – a synonym he clearly expected others to understand – Abdera's greatest distinction was its philosophers. (Perhaps Cicero *was* thinking about the philosophers?) The greatest of these was Democritus (b. *c.* 460 BC). Unless one gives credit to the scarcely known Leucippus – perhaps from Miletus – Democritus is the originator of the ancient atomic theory that accounted for the processes of the natural world (see Part II, Ch. 7). The other Abderan philosopher is Protagoras (485–411 BC), one of the best known of the Sophists. His quotation, 'Man is the measure of all things', is as well known as it is obscure. In his dialogue the *Theaetetus*, Plato tries to unpack Protagoras' idea thus:

SOCRATES. Man, Protagoras says, 'is the measure of all things, of the existence of things that are, and of the non-existence of things that are not'. You have read him?

THEAETETUS. Oh yes, many times.

SOCRATES. Does he not mean that things are to you such as they appear to you, and to me such as they appear to me, and that you and I are men?

THEAETETUS. Yes. He says that.

SOCRATES. A wise man is not likely to talk nonsense. Let us try to understand him. The same wind is blowing, yet one of us is cold and the other not. Is the wind in itself cold … or is it as each feels it to be?

It is at least a beautifully provoking philosophical question originating in an Abderan.

Acragas
This city – the Roman Agrigentum, modern Agrigento – was a Hellenic colony founded in southern Sicily in about 580 BC. Its early prosperity is clear from the magnificent temples that still mark it as among the most impressive of Greek ruins. It was much damaged during the wars between Rome and Carthage, but it recovered. After the fall of the Roman Empire in the West (AD 410, and finally in AD 476), the city shrank to a mere settlement on the old acropolis.

For a period in the 5th century BC, Acragas had a limited demo-cratic government in which Empedocles (c. 492–432 BC), the Presocratic philosopher who was much influenced by Pythagoras, Parmenides and Xenophanes, was conspicuous.

Alexandria
Founded in 331 BC by Alexander the Great, the city was made their capital by the Ptolemies, his successors in Egypt. Initially, and at intervals later on, Alexandria had a democratic government on the Hellenistic pattern. Its population, which eventually reached half a million or more, made it for four hundred years the second city of the Roman Empire. It continued to prosper as a centre of Christian organ-ization until it was taken decisively by the Arabs in 640 AD.

It is not for the people who were born or educated there – with the conspicuous exception of Plotinus (205–269 AD), the founder of Neoplatonism (see Part II, Ch. 9) – that Alexandria is famous in the history of ideas, but for its two great institutions, the museum and the library, and for the scholars, scientists and mathematicians who were attracted to the place as a consequence.

The museum, which in organization and activity was as close as antiquity got to a modern university or research institute, was established and sustained by Ptolemy I and II, the immediate successors of Alexander; it was supported generously by their dynasty (of whom Cleopatra was the last) and by the Roman emperors, particularly Hadrian. There were salaried scholars, a president or head, and learned dinners (symposia) that attracted the powerful and erudite – including Plutarch, Lucian and Galen, among many others. The museum was probably terminated by Theodosius I in or around AD 391 as part of his imposition of dogmatic Christianity on the Eastern Roman Empire.

The library, also established by the Ptolemies, was a separate institution. It was probably located near the museum in the palace area, and it was reputed to hold an immense collection, perhaps as many as half a million rolls (the equivalent of some 100,000 modern books). Its closest rival, at Pergamon, contained a mere 200,000 rolls, but these Hellenistic libraries established the precedent for Roman private and public libraries – all of which were prey to fire, mould, worm and, later, to the destructive activity of the new religions. The Alexandrian library was accidentally burnt in 48/47 BC, when Julius Caesar was besieging the palace area, but it seems to have been partially restored.

Ancient Alexandria lies mostly beneath the modern city; the Hellenistic and Roman remains that can be seen today are some 5.5 metres (18 feet) or more below street level. The sites of the museum and library have yet to be established, but as Professor Richard Sorabji reported informally in a lecture note of August 2009:

All twenty stone-built lecture rooms of the Alexandrian multi-disciplinary school in which Philoponus [490–570 AD; a distinguished Christian Neoplatonist] taught have been excavated in the last few years. They are so astonishingly complete that we can get a picture of how different advanced teaching was then. The professor sat on a throne at the back of a horseshoe of stone seats that would accommodate at least 30 pupils. The curve was designed so that professor and students could all see each other. But at the open mouth of the horseshoe, the person (student under critical examination?) addressing the seminar stood in a most exposed position at a lectern. The hole for the lectern survives in one of the stone blocks that are positioned there.

Aphrodisias

The site of Aphrosias is due east of Ephesus and about 230 km (145 miles) south-east of Smyrna (Izmir) in modern Turkey. Apart from the acropolis, it occupies a flat area that is drained by the Meander river system. The ruins are magnificent, and the stadium, almost complete, is one of the most impressive to be seen anywhere. There is a well-written and illustrated guide to the site by K. T. Erim.

The city was in the ancient cultural and political area of Asia Minor known as Caria. From earlier small settlements, it began to develop substantially in the 2nd century BC. It sided with Rome against Mithridates of Pontus in 88 BC, and as a consequence gained privileges and freedoms that persisted for more than three hundred years.

Celebrated Aphrodisians include Chariton, the author of *Callirhoe,* the earliest novel that survives from antiquity. Dating from somewhere between 50 BC and AD 100, it is full of the travels, presumed deaths, pirates, shipwrecks, enslavements, love affairs and happy endings that came to characterize the genre. Adrastus, a minor exponent of Aristotle's writings, was also born in the city, in the 2nd century AD, as was the more significant Alexander of Aphrodisias – a distinguished commentator on Aristotle who flourished *c.* AD 210. Some of his writings survive in Greek, but others were translated into Arabic and indeed still exist only in that language.

Assos

Assos is on the shore of modern Turkey where the coast of the Aegean runs east–west along the south of the Troad. To the north is the large and legendary range of hills that culminates in Mount Ida. To the south, a mere 11 km (7 miles) away, is the Greek island of Lesbos. Assos was in fact established by colonists from the city of Methymna on Lesbos, in the 7th century BC. Despite its once important position astride the coastal road, its strong defensive position, and its brief significance in the history of scientific enquiry (*c.* 340 BC), Assos played no important part in history, instead following the ups and downs of almost all Ionian cities: freedom, Persian domination, semi-autonomy under a satrap, Alexandrian 'liberation', subjection to the rule of Alexander's often conflicting successors, Roman rule drifting into Byzantine dominion, and finally abandonment under the Ottomans.

Extensive remains are visible, including walls of the 4th century BC, but the crowning glory of the site is the unusually early (6th-century BC) temple to Athena Polias, where many of the primitive Doric columns have been re-erected. From here, the modern tourist, if he or she is still able to stand (or has been re-erected by a guide after the climb) can experience glorious views across to Lesbos. Those who venture there alone may perhaps still feel the power of an Aeolian sanctuary, or *temenos*, where men once encountered their gods.

Assos was the birthplace of the Stoic philosopher Cleanthes (331–232 BC), a pupil of Stoicism's founder, Zeno, and his successor as head of the Stoa in Athens (see Part II, Ch. 8). A little earlier, and more importantly, Hermias – a former student at Plato's Academy and a contemporary there of Aristotle – became the ruler, under nominal Persian suzerainty, of an area that included Assos. On Plato's death, he invited Aristotle (384–322 BC) to settle there with his younger fellow student and friend Theophrastus (372–287 BC). It was on the adjacent sea shore (and in the two great bays of Lesbos that teem with marine life – or did, until they were over-fished in the 1990s), in the years 347–345, that Aristotle, Theophrastus and their students collected, dissected and categorized hundreds of specimens according to anatomical functions, thus beginning the sciences of marine biology, zoology and botany (see Part II, Ch. 6). They carried out their research with such excellence that no significant improvements were made for about two thousand years. (See also **Lesbos**.)

Athens

In Classical antiquity – say, from 547 BC, when the Persians arrived in Asia Minor, to about AD 529, the closure of the philosophical schools in Athens – there was almost no one of cultural, scientific or philosophical importance who did not at some time live in, visit or have dealings with Alexandria, Rome or Constantinople. But the most persistent of these ancient cultural centres was Athens. Of the great philosophers, only Socrates (469–399 BC), who came from a *deme* (township) subject to Athens, and Plato (427–347 BC), who was born to an aristocratic Athenian family, were citizens. Aristotle studied at Plato's Academy between 367 and 347, and later returned to Athens to teach and establish his own philosophical school, the Lyceum, but he was not a citizen.

The intellectual pre-eminence of Athens was secured by its political importance and by the teaching institutions set up by Plato and Aristotle, and also, within thirty years of Aristotle's death, the Stoa of the Stoics and the Garden of the Epicureans. The Academy survived in various forms until AD 529. Indeed, it is only recently that archaeologists have unearthed two house foundations that are almost certainly the last residence of the school of Damascius, one of the seven free-thinking philosophers expelled by Justinian in 529 and given sanctuary by the king of Persia.

Athens is often visited via its port at Piraeus – once connected to the city by a long line of fortified walls, but now by a haphazard concrete confusion. The Acropolis is still awesome, despite centuries of neglect and pillage, and the Parthenon remains forever the most perfectly proportioned colonnaded building in the world. The new museum below the Acropolis is excellent but should be visited with a good guide.

Histories and guidebooks to Athens are legion: take your pick! The earliest, and one of the most intriguing, is Book I of Pausanias' *Descriptions of Greece* – a mixture of history and accurate topography for Roman tourists written at the height of Pax Romana in the 2nd century AD. It is available at a moderate price in the admirable Loeb Classical Library (Cambridge, Mass., 1913).

Chalcedon

Chalcedon is of no interest except as the birthplace of Thrasymachus, a Sophist who flourished *c.* 430–400 BC and is famous for his defence, in Plato's *Republic*, of the power-politics view that justice is whatever is in the interests of the stronger.

The city itself was founded on the Asiatic side of the Bosphorus in about 685 BC, when the better site on the European side was still empty (Byzantium was established there seventeen years later). So ill-judged was the choice of location that Herodotus, writing in about 440 BC, remarks that 'the Chalcedonians must have been blind at the time'. Whatever may remain is now buried under the suburbs of Istanbul.

Chios

The birthplace of Homer, who was always represented as blind, was claimed by no fewer than seven Hellenic cities, but the large island of

Chios has the most interesting and longest-maintained claim to an honour that can never be awarded. Its nearest rival was Smyrna (modern Izmir), but the island's claim is enshrined in an ancient 'Hymn to Apollo', dating from about 560 BC, which the Chians took as decisive:

> Who was the sweetest singer of them all?
> Who made your hearts most rejoice? Tell them:
> 'A blind man who dwells on rocky Chios was the sweetest singer;
> His verses are the noblest of all, and will live for ever.'

What is more certain is that Chios was the birthplace of Ion (*c.* 480–421 BC), a prolific poet, author and playwright who was second only to the greatest Athenian writers. His works, save for fragments, are lost.

Apart from its still wild and always beautiful mountains, among the island's surviving gems are the two villages of Mesta and Pergi. Mesta is famous for its medieval wall of fortified houses and its narrow, labyrinthine streets, many of which are vaulted over; Pergi, on the other hand, is noted for its narrow compression and its unique *sgraffito* decoration, consisting of grey and white semi-geometrical patterns on the houses' exteriors. But there is another remote place, the Nea Moni monastery. Go there, alone if you can. It is far from the madding crowd and almost abandoned by worldly religion, but an aura of peace and ancient holiness lingers there and holds the pilgrim, much as the sacred spaces of other, older, long-departed religions must in their day have held the suppliant at Assos and Carthage, Karnak and Avebury, Babylon and Delphi.

Clazomenae

Clazomenae is on the coast of the Aegean, about 37 km (23 miles) west of Smyrna (Izmir) in modern Turkey. Owing to the depredations of Byzantine and Ottoman builders, only the scantiest remains are now visible to the non-archaeologist on its island site, which was once joined to the mainland by a causeway. See G. E. Bean, *Aegean Turkey* (London, revd edn 1989), for a readable account.

The city claims two philosophers as its citizens: Anaxagoras (*c.* 500–426 BC), who was the first philosopher to settle in Athens, and Scopelianus, an insignificant Sophist of the 2nd century AD.

Cnidus

Cnidus, often spelt Knidos (closer to the original Greek), had among its citizens the outstanding mathematician and astronomer Eudoxus (*c.* 390–340 BC), and Sostratus, who designed the Pharos lighthouse at Alexandria. Built 300–280 BC, it measured 100 metres (328 feet) high, and lasted until it was brought down by an earthquake in AD 1326.

The Cnidus you will see was established in the period 350–310 BC by the removal of an earlier foundation ('Old Cnidus') from the south coast of the Gulf of Syme, about 32 km (20 miles) to the east. The newer city is on the extreme south-west tip of the long peninsula that divides the Mediterranean from the Aegean. No modern developments or dwellings intrude upon the ruins, and neither of the two harbours (north and south of the quasi-island that ends the peninsula) can accommodate any of the floating hotels that pass as boats in so many Mediterranean ports.

The remains are extensive and the site beautiful. Modern archaeologists have identified the base of the *tholos* (a circular building often ringed with pillars) where the most celebrated sculpture of antiquity drew throngs of Greek and Roman tourists: the Aphrodite (Diana) of Praxiteles, who lived between about 375 and 330 BC. The Cnidians purchased the statue almost as soon as the city was moved to its present site, where it commands the coastal trade route from the Levant and Egypt to the Hellenic world. Lucian's dialogue *Amores* ('Loves'), probably written after 200 AD, is an amusing and refreshing take on homosexuality, as well as a fascinating account of the statue and its environs that can still be used as you look at the site today. See the Loeb Classical Library's edition of *Lucian*, vol. VIII (Cambridge, Mass., 1967). Praxiteles' statue is lost, although copies give us some idea of its appearance.

Colophon

At its zenith, before the coming of the Persians in 545 BC, Colophon was the birthplace of one whose name is always noted in mankind's attempts to understand the nature of the universe, even though only fragments of his writings survive. He is Xenophanes (see Part II, Ch. 4): the first to have speculated about a cosmic god having no human or animal form. He was also a poet, and apparently the first to have thought systematically about the distinction between opinion and knowledge. He was born between 580 and 560 BC, and left Colophon at the coming of the Persians.

The city itself occupied a hill on the north side of the Meander, north-west of Ephesus. It was notorious (envied?) for the extravagant life-style of its inhabitants, but its significance declined in the centuries following the Persian invasion. Eventually its very name was transferred to the settlement of Notium, a few miles away on the coast, which became 'New Colophon'. As the travel writer Freya Stark has observed, 'Of the ancient city nothing, not even the name, is left – except a few dim heavings of disintegrated walls on a steep and ruinous hillside thickly overgrown' (*Ionia: A Quest*; London, 1954). But a nearby site, belonging to Colophon, is well worth seeing and is still being actively examined by archaeologists. It is the oracular Temple of Apollo at Claros, south of Colophon and about one mile inland from Notium.

When you visit this place, recall the words of the Roman historian Tacitus, writing in about AD 100: 'Here a male priest … hears the names of the consultants and their number, but no more, then descends into a cavern, swallows a draught of water from a mysterious spring, and – though generally ignorant of writing and metre – delivers his response in set verses dealing with the subject each enquirer had in mind' (*Annals* II.54). Note well that he *descends*.

Croton *see* **Elea**

Cyrene
Cyrene, the major Greek colony on the North African coast (now in Libya), was established in about 630 BC and gave its name to the surrounding area, Cyrenaica. Despite losing its independence successively to Persia, the Ptolemies of Egypt and Rome, and being subject to attack from the sea by pirates and from the Libyan hinterland, it was a successful city for much of the Classical and Hellenistic periods, even surviving for a time after the Arab invasions of the 7th century.

Among other figures, the city produced one name of doubtful repute: Aristippus, an associate of Socrates who is represented by Xenophon as a self-indulgent pleasure seeker. It also produced two great men. The first was Callimachus, who flourished 285–240 BC and was one of the finest and most prolific of Greek poets, working mostly in Alexandria.

Only a tiny fraction of his poetry survives, but this includes the lines immortally rendered into English by W. J. Cory that begin: 'They told me, Heraclitus, they told me you were dead.' The second figure was Carneades (c. 214–129 BC), who became head of Plato's Academy in Athens during its 'sceptical' period – that is to say, when it was more concerned with the development of critical philosophical techniques (compare Oxford in the 1950s) than with the discussion or propagation of any particular philosopher's ideas. Carneades was a formidable critic of the Stoic and Epicurean philosophies, as he was of any positive opinions. He enjoyed a high reputation but left no writings: his arguments were reported by his pupils and opponents.

Elea

Founded as a colony from the southern Greek mainland in about 540 BC, Elea is situated on the Italian coast about 60 kilometres (36 miles) south of the famous temples at Paestum. Its modern name is Castellamare. It is one of the many Greek colonies established between the 7th and 5th centuries BC that formed what is known as *Magna Graecia* (in Greek, *Megale Hellas*). As well as Elea, these included the cities of Neapolis (Naples), Tarentum (Tarento), Croton (modern Crotone, on the southeast coast of the toe of Italy), Sybaris (north of Croton, from which English acquired the word 'sybaritic') and, in Sicily, Acragas and Syracuse (scene of Athens' dreadful defeat in 413 BC by Spartan allies in the Peloponnesian War, and later the home of Archimedes, the greatest mathematician of antiquity).

These colonies were associated with two highly influential strands in the web of Greek and much subsequent thinking: the Pythagorean and the Eleatic, or Parmenidean. Pythagoras was born on Samos but migrated to Croton somewhere about 530 BC (see Part II, Ch. 4). Parmenides of Elea, who flourished about 480 BC, was the first philosopher to raise serious (and perhaps insoluble) problems about the nature of change. His questions were sharpened by Zeno, also from Elea, by means of several paradoxes of division that still alarm today (see Part II, Ch. 4).

Ephesus

For all its antiquity and importance as a Hellenistic city, and later as the seat of the Roman governor of Asia Minor, Ephesus did not sustain any significant school of philosophy or tradition of scientific learning. But it did produce one name of renown among the Presocratic philosophers: Heraclitus the Dark. The aphoristic fragments of his work that survive extend to about eight pages of modern print. They are interrelated, dense, enigmatic, authoritarian and provocative. The best known, but not the best, are versions of the saying: 'No man steps into the same river twice.' Heraclitus flourished in about 480 BC (see Part II, Ch. 4).

The ruins of Hellenistic, Roman and Byzantine Ephesus as they exist today are visited by tens of thousands of tourists each year. With a few ugly exceptions, the reconstructions are very fine, particularly the Library of Celsus and one of the theatres. The terraced houses, roofed over for their own protection, rival those of Pompeii and are supremely well worth a visit, even with the extra charge involved. The big disappointment is the sunken oblong area where the Temple of Artemis – one of the seven wonders of the ancient world – once stood. It is badly presented and gives little idea of the wonderful scale of the building. The reduction of this great structure to a weed-grown void was effected partly by acts of God, in the form of earthquakes, and partly by acts of men, in the form of Christians. As an otherwise unknown early Christian wrote: 'It is now the most desolate and the most wretched ⌈of places⌉ through the grace of Christ and John the Theologian.'

Ephesus: The New Guide, edited by P. Scherrer and authorized by the Austrian Institute of Archaeology (Istanbul, 2000), is excellent. The museum contains some superb finds, including the 'lesser' Artemis – the power of whose face, once seen, is never likely to be forgotten. There is also a fine and almost perfect bust of the Stoic emperor Marcus Aurelius.

Halicarnassus

Visitors to south-west Turkey can scarcely avoid Halicarnassus (modern Bodrum), be they tourists, sailors or air travellers. Over the past fifty years the modern city has spread its concrete fingers up the surrounding slopes, and the ancient city is now the commercial hinterland to a large marina. The excavated footings of the great funeral temple to Mausolus (the original Mausoleum) – the only elements the Crusaders could not remove to build their castle – can still be seen. The city walls that existed when Ada, Mausolus' sister, judiciously 'adopted'

Alexander the Great can still be traced by the dedicated antiquarian. The theatre has gone, and the site of the marketplace is untraceable, but what can never be lost is the fame of the two great historians who were born here. They are Herodotus (c. 490–425 BC) and Dionysius of Halicarnassus, who lived in Rome from about 30 BC until after AD 8.

Herodotus, the first-known critical historian, gives us a priceless supply of information about the Persian Wars and the state of the Eastern Mediterranean in the 5th century BC. Despite the loss of the later books of his lengthy *Roman Antiquities*, Dionysius provides much detail about early Roman history.

Have a look at the Crusader castle. There is a good open-air fish restaurant on the way.

Herculaneum

Herculaneum, on the coast about 8 km (5 miles) south-east of the centre of modern Naples, is perhaps best regarded as an affluent suburb of Pompeii, whose fate it shared in the eruption of Vesuvius in AD 79. The volcanic ash that covered Herculaneum solidified into hard rock, permitting some of the slums of Naples to be built above. The visitor can now walk down a steep slope to the partially excavated level of the Roman town and the old seashore. What the visitor cannot see properly is the literary and cultural treasure that remains partially entombed: the extensive house known as 'The Villa of the Papyri'. This structure contains the library of Philodemus, or at least some of his books. He was an important Epicurean philosopher and poet, and worked there at least between 75 and 50 BC. He was born at Gadara in Syria about 110 BC and died about 35 BC. Unfortunately, the hundreds of papyrus rolls recovered from the villa were carbonized by the heat of the volcanic ash and look like lumps of coal. But limitless patience, academic skill, and modern electronic aids that allow researchers to trace the remains of the ink lettering have resulted in the recovery of lost works, the writings of Philodemus himself, Epicurus and the Stoic Chrysippus among them. Those of us who are young may live long enough to read significant parts of the lost thoughts of antiquity, in particular Epicurus' masterwork *On Nature*. Those of us who are old can only regret, in the odd way familiar to human nature, that we will never see what we are so soon destined to forget for ever.

Kos

The quiet and historically inconspicuous island of Kos (or Cos) lies west of the Ceramic Gulf, the last and longest-protruding inlet of the sea on the south-west corner of mainland Turkey. Ancient Halicarnassus (now Bodrum) lay a few miles along its northern side. Kos has one, not very well validated, claim to distinction: it is supposedly the birthplace of Hippocrates, 'the father of medicine' (*c.* 460–370 BC) and the area where he practised. Quite apart from his medical prescriptions (or 'their' medical prescriptions: his works are in fact a later collection of treatises on Hippocratic medicine), the oath that is always associated with Hippocrates still expresses the ethics of the good physician. It is so often referred to, and so difficult to locate, that I shall give it here almost in its entirety. It begins: 'I swear by Apollo the Physician and by Asclepius … to honour my teachers and share in learning with my fellow physicians', and then continues:

> I will use regimes for the benefit of the ill in accordance with my ability and judgement, but from what is to their harm or injustice I shall keep them. And I shall not give a drug that is deadly to anyone if asked for it [i.e. a poison: this is not necessarily an oath against euthanasia]. Nor will I suggest the way to such a counsel. And likewise I will not give a woman a destructive pessary … I will not cut, and certainly not those suffering from stone, but I will cede this to men who are practitioners of this activity [i.e. surgeons]. Into as many houses as I may enter, I will go for the benefit of the ill, while being far from all voluntary and destructive injustices, especially from sexual acts both upon women's bodies and upon men's, both of the free and of slaves. And about whatever I may see or hear in treatment, or even outside treatment, in the life of human beings – things that should never be let slip outside – I shall remain silent, holding such things sacred and not to be divulged.

Whether or not Hippocrates was from Kos, it is certain that the island contained one of the great healing places of antiquity. This was an area of temples and terraces sacred to the kindly god of healing,

Asclepius (in Latin, Aesculapius). Judging on the evidence of inscribed votive offerings, as well as general repute and the written reports of Aelius Aristides, a successful hypochondriac of the 2nd century AD, the god's successes were on a par with the healings at Lourdes, and probably derived from a similar combination of faith, hope and a little gentle medical attention.

The Asclepium is a few miles out of Kos town. The terraces rise into a background of pine-clad hills and face across the sea to Asia Minor. The place is still redolent of peace and healing. A masterpiece of Hellenistic architecture before its spoliation, the site is dominated by the great staircase that leads to the crowning Doric temple of the 2nd century BC. (See also Pergamon.)

Lesbos

Lesbos is the third-largest of the Greek islands, after Crete and Euboea. It is situated a few miles off the Turkish mainland, west of Pergamon and south of Assos. Several mountains are over 900 metres (nearly 3,000 feet), and much of the lower land is exceptionally fertile. The two most interesting features in terms of geography and the origins of the biological sciences are the large gulfs of Kalloni and Gera, the latter forming almost a lagoon. The island has an interesting history of semi-independence throughout antiquity, and was conspicuous for its seaborne commerce; but its principal claim to fame is as the birthplace of Sappho (b. *c.* 612 BC) and of one of Classical antiquity's greatest philosopher–scientists, Theophrastus (372–287 BC; see Part II, Ch. 6).

Judging by comments about her and quotations in ancient sources, Sappho must have been a prolific as well as an outstanding poet. Now only two complete poems survive, together with numerous small items that were mostly found in the 20th century on Egyptian papyri. She created personal love lyrics of great intensity, often addressed to women, but never referring to physical relations. The poet Anacreon (born in Teos about 570 BC) is perhaps the source of the still prevailing usage that associates the name of the island with female homosexuality.

Theophrastus was a student of Plato's at the Academy, where his sojourn overlapped with that of Aristotle's. The two became colleagues in their investigations of marine biology in the Gulf of Gera, and Theophrastus went on to succeed Aristotle as the head of the Lyceum –

Aristotle's research institute. He was a major contributor to the biological sciences in his own right, and produced the first typography of human characteristics of the sort we now call psychological. He would be better known but for the loss of most of his works and the misfortune of being so close to the colossal figure of Aristotle (see Part II, Ch. 5).

Epicurus taught for a period, possibly at a school (gymnasium) at Mytilene in about 318 BC.

Miletus

The city is on what is now an inland site about 50 km (30 miles) south of Ephesus. The river Meander has washed down such deposits of earth and sand in the last three thousand years that what was once a magnificent sea port is now a low hill 15 km (9 miles) from the sea, at the edge of a large and ill-defined area of brackish marsh and flat agricultural land. The modern road runs straight across this reclaimed land towards the spectacular theatre finished in the Roman style in about AD 100. (The seating area is a near-perfect half-circle rather than the original Hellenic horseshoe.) It requires an effort of the imagination to see all the surrounding area as sea and the main harbour of Miletus as an inlet to the left of and behind the theatre as you face it. The final decline caused by this silting probably began in the mid-3rd century AD. The origins of Miletus are very remote, stretching back long before the presumed date of the Trojan War, in about 1250 BC. Homer named the city as an ally of Troy. In the 7th and 6th centuries BC, it developed a powerful navy and established settlements and trading stations on the Euxine (Black) Sea and on Propontis (the Sea of Marmara), so that Herodotus could describe it as 'at the height of its fortune and the chief ornament of Ionia'. Even when Croesus ('As rich as Croesus'), the last king of Lydia in the middle years of the 6th century BC, took more or less benign control of most of Ionia, Miletus remained independent. Similarly, when the Persian king Cyrus deposed Croesus in about 546, Miletus still retained partial control of its own affairs until its ill-advised instigation of the Ionian Revolt against the Persians in 499. The uprising ended in disaster with the naval battle of Lade in 494. (Lade, formerly an island, is now a bump in the silted-up sea around Miletus.) The Persians destroyed Miletus after the sea battle, and the oracular sanctuary of Didyma, 16 km (10 miles) south of the city and connected to it by a sacred road, was burnt. The ruins now visible at Didyma – one of the most awesome places of the ancient world – are of the 'new' temple commenced in about 300 BC.

Following the Persian reprisals, Miletus was rebuilt but never regained the power it had before 546. It suffered the familiar Ionian see-saw of Persian and Athenian domination until it was forcibly 'liberated' by Alexander the Great after dithering about whether to support the Persians or the Macedonian Greeks. It became part of the Roman province of Asia in 129 BC. Many of the extant ruins are Hellenistic – for example the council chamber – but most are Roman or Roman overlay on Hellenistic originals. St Paul visited the city in AD 51, and Apollo performed a miracle at Didyma when the Goths invaded Asia Minor and attacked Miletus in AD 263. A Byzantine fort now sits behind, and partly on top of, the theatre. There are no modern developments.

The extraordinary speculations of Thales, Anaximander and Anaximenes that began the scientific questioning of nature all date to the great age of Miletus, between about 625 BC and 546 BC (see Part II, Ch. 3). A little later the city produced Hecataeus, who flourished about 500 BC. He was one of the earliest composers of a historical geography of the Mediterranean coast, and a cautious-minded man: 'I write what seems to me to be true; for the Hellenes have many tales which appear to me to be foolishness.' Miletus also lays claim to Hippodamus – the town-planner of Piraeus – whose grid system for streets can be discerned in Priene, New York, and still (faintly) behind the theatre in Miletus itself. The city may, just possibly, have been the early home of the almost legendary Leucippus, the ultimate source, behind Democritus, of the atomic theory.

Miletus is so interesting as a place to visit, and so much involved in the beginnings of European science, that it is worth reproducing an ancient account of the place. It is given by the Graeco-Roman geographer Strabo (64 BC–*c.* AD 21):

> Miletus was first founded and fortified above the sea by the Cretans, where Miletus of olden times is now situated … but later Neleus and his followers fortified the present city …
> The present city has four harbours, one of which is large enough for a fleet … The Euxine Sea [Black Sea] had been colonized

everywhere by these peoples, as also Propontis [Sea of Marmara]
… Notable men were born at Miletus: Thales, one of the seven
wise men, the first to begin the study of nature and mathematics
among the Hellenes, and his pupil Anaximander, and again the
pupil of the latter, Anaximenes, and also Hecataeus, the author
of the historical geography … But the city was unfortunate,
since it shut its gates against Alexander and was taken by force,
as was also the case with Halicarnassus; and also, before that
time, it was taken by the Persian.

This quotation is taken from Book XIV of Strabo's *Geography*. Books
XIII and XIV (found together in vol. VI of the Loeb Classical Library's
excellent edition of Strabo's works) contain fascinating contemporary
descriptions of many of the places and sites visible today from Troy to
Rhodes and eastwards. Highly recommended!

Oinoanda

Oinoanda (the *oi* is pronounced as in *boy*) is somewhat difficult to find
on or off the map, and can scarcely be found at all in books, ancient or
modern. It is situated about 20 km (12½ miles) north-east of Fethiye,
above the village of Incealiler, near where the Fethiye–Sogut road
crosses the river Xanthus. It seems to have had no history before the
2nd century BC and, although some handsome sections of Hellenistic
walls remain, its principal fortifications were constructed later, when
the Pax Romana was beginning to break down and Gothić invasion
was a threat.

The climb up to the city is steep, stony and long. The oblong site,
crowning the hill, is overgrown, earthquake-tumbled and precipitous,
but wildly beautiful. As you approach the top, following the left-hand
path from Incealiler, do not be deceived by the first wall you must
scramble over. It is not the city wall, but the aqueduct approaching
from the south. More archaeological explorations are pending, and
armed guards patrol to prevent looting.

No one of any significance ever came from Oinoanda, but something of unique philosophical importance was done here. In about
AD 130 a certain Diogenes of Oinoanda caused an inscription amount-
ing to about 25,000 words to be carved on a wall, probably in the agora.

It is the last authoritative exposition of the Epicurean philosophy to be recorded in antiquity. It survived for perhaps 150 years before the stones were reused in the late fortifications and in other buildings. These fragments now lie scattered and jumbled, lost, broken and buried: the heaviest and most important jigsaw puzzle in the world. About 6,000 words have been retrieved, much of it by Professor Martin Smith of Durham University (see Part II, Ch. 7).

Pergamon

Although a city of considerable wealth and importance in the Hellenistic and Roman world, with library, schools and great civic buildings, Pergamon boasts only one really famous son: Galen (AD 129–?199/216), the great anatomist, physician and polymath. At the height of his career he was court physician to the emperor Marcus Aurelius. Julianus, the future emperor and last articulate and powerful opponent of Christianity, studied Neoplatonism at Pergamon for a period after AD 351.

Pergamon (modern Bergama) is situated on the Turkish mainland directly east of Lesbos and about 27 km (17 miles) inland. It is first mentioned in Greek literature in connection with the year 400 BC, at the very end of Xenophon's *Anabasis* – his vivid account of how 10,000 Greek mercenaries were extracted from a desperate situation in Mesopotamia via eastern Anatolia and the Black Sea. The travel writer Freya Stark tells the story succinctly: 'When Xenophon arrived at Pergamon in the destitute condition which anyone who has travelled about in Asia will probably sympathize with, he was instigated by his hostess and encouraged by omens to attempt the capture of a Persian who lived with his family and property in the plain below' (*Ionia: A Quest*; London, 1954). The outcome was not as anticipated. The Persian survived, and Xenophon went home to Athens none the richer.

The city was fully and expensively Hellenized by Eumenes II (r. 197–159 BC), when it formed one of the small but rich kingdoms established after the redistribution of Alexander's empire. Although politically subservient to Ephesus in the Roman period, Pergamon continued to develop magnificent public buildings – baths, temples, walls and markets – many of which survive as substantial ruins, but the visitor has to divert to Berlin to see the best piece of all, the great Altar of Zeus.

The Asclepium (see under **Kos**) is below and a little distance from the main city. It is a large area that includes a hospital, temple, colonnade, small theatre and stadium – a veritable health centre of the Classical world.

Priene

No person of consequence in the history of the world – Hellenistic or otherwise – has ever come from Priene. But it is worth a visit for two reasons.

One is that its site, on an elevated position above the silted-up estuary of the Meander, looking across the sea-like flatness of fields to Miletus in the south-west, gives a superb prospect of what it once looked like – providing you can imagine sea in place of flat land.

The other reason is that Priene provides one of the best-presented examples anywhere of a Hellenistic city (see Part I, Ch. 2). The Romans largely abandoned it to a fate of isolated unimportance, but archaeologists have now removed the Byzantine rubble that cluttered its original streets, revealing their clear Hippodamian grid pattern (see **Miletus**). The houses are uniform and of moderate size; and everything that would be expected of an aspiring Hellenistic city is in place: temple, theatre, stadium, council chamber, agora, city walls and an all but inaccessible acropolis.

Why was Priene so little developed after the 2nd century BC? Almost certainly because it lost its harbour, and therefore its trade and communication route, to the silt of the Meander about four hundred years earlier than the similar strangulation of Miletus. The old harbour has not been found. It must be somewhere below the flat fields that lap the foot of the inland hill that is Priene today.

Rhodes

The history of Rhodes, the large Greek island close to the south-western part of modern Turkey anciently known as Caria, can be traced back to the Minoan (Cretan) settlements of the 16th century BC. From then on it followed a familiar pattern: Mycenaean colonization, Dark Age settlement by the Dorian Greeks (who themselves went on to colonize elsewhere), the development of independent city states (originally three in the case of Rhodes), submission to Persia in 490 BC, alternate alliance and misalliance with Athens and Sparta, an on–off independence from the successors of Alexander the Great, initial cooperation with Rome, then equivocal cooperation, and finally alliance with the great power in 164 BC, under whose suzerainty Rhodes prospered with a partly democratic government.

Before 408 BC, when a federal state was established with Rhodes itself as its main city, Rhodes the island had three distinct city states: Lindus, Ialysus and Camirus. The ancient city of Rhodes is now mostly under the medieval mass of the fortress of the Knights of St John, but parts of the walls, the acropolis and the necropolis can still be seen.

Apollonius Rhodius may have been born on the island; he certainly lived there for a significant period before settling in Alexandria, where he became one of the librarians of the Library between 270 and about 245 BC. He is author of the celebrated epic the *Argonautica* – the much-replayed and Hollywood-enhanced story of Jason and his quest for the Golden Fleece.

In the history of ideas, Rhodes is famous as the location of a major school of Stoic philosophy (see Part II, Ch. 8). The great Panaetius (c. 185–109 BC) came from the island, although he lived mostly in Rome or Athens. By the end of the 2nd century BC, Rhodes the city had become the leading centre of Stoicism. Posidonius (c. 135–51 BC) taught there: his pupils included Cicero, to whom we owe so much of what survives of quotations from his teachers. (Incidentally, Cicero is the first man whose dates of birth and death we know exactly: 3 January 106 and 7 December 43 BC.) Not only Cicero, but many other Romans came to Rhodes to complete their education, much as the rich and able still flood to Harvard or Oxford from abroad – partly for educational purposes, partly in order to say that they have been there.

Rome

In the origin and transmission of world-changing philosophical and scientific ideas, five names are most easily associated with Rome. They are Cicero (106–43 BC), Lucretius (c. 98–c. 55 BC), Seneca (c. 4 BC–AD 65), Epictetus (c. AD 50–c. 120) and Marcus Aurelius (AD 120–180).

To Marcus Tullius Cicero, orator, statesman, politician and writer, we owe an enormous debt of gratitude for recording, for the first time in Latin, the philosophical ideas and arguments of Greek philosophers in the 2nd century BC that would otherwise be lost. To fill in the time (!), in the final three years of his life he produced seven books: *Academica*, mainly concerning the arguments of Carneades and the Academy of Plato in its 'sceptical' period; *De finibus*, on philosophers' different views of about the 'chief good'; *Tusculan Disputations*, concerning the nature of happiness; *De natura deorum*, on Stoic, Epicurean and Sceptic accounts of the nature and existence of God or gods; *De fato* ('On fate'); *De divinatione* ('On divination'); and *De officiis* ('On duties'). The whole is a priceless resource of information and much of it surprisingly readable. Try the *De natura deorum*: nothing as open-minded and well balanced would be written again in Europe until David Hume's *Dialogues Concerning Natural Religion* was published in 1779. Hume took Cicero as his model.

Lucretius is the author of what is arguably the most influential poem ever written, namely the full and splendid account of Epicurean atomism entitled *De rerum natura* (usually translated as 'On the nature of the universe'; see Part II, Ch. 7).

Seneca and Marcus Aurelius, at different times respectively the chief administrator of the Roman empire and its emperor, provide remarkable and intimate accounts of how Stoicism can be applied in real life, even in positions of ultimate human power. Epictetus, a freed slave, lectured on Stoicism in Rome.

Many millions of words have been written on Rome and its history. Read more: Edward Gibbon's *The Decline and Fall of the Roman Empire* is still one of the greatest reads in the English language.

Samos

The island of Samos nurtured two men whose names are known almost everywhere, and a third who could have been more famous than Copernicus. The first is the legendary Pythagoras (b. *c.* 570 BC), who was very probably born on Samos but migrated to Elea in Magna Graecia, where his influence seems to have been profound and long lasting (see Part II, Ch. 4). The second is Epicurus (341–*c.* 270 BC), who was born on Samos, the son of a schoolmaster who had Athenian citizenship. He settled in Athens in 307 BC (see Part II, Ch. 7). The third man is the astronomer Aristarchus (320 – well after 280 BC). According to the remarkable book on large numbers known as *The Sand-Reckoner*, written by Archimedes of Syracuse (d. 212 BC), Aristarchus was the first known person to propose 'that the universe is many times greater in size than the universe so called. His hypotheses are that the fixed stars and the sun remain motionless, that the earth itself revolves [and moves] in the circumference of a circle about the sun.' Revolutionary scientific ideas need to be sown in an environment that can support them, and Aristarchus' hypothesis arrived too early. It made calculation difficult, and the rotation of the earth appeared to be incompatible with experience (it was not evident that the atmosphere turned with the earth).

Samos is an island of about 471 square km (182 sq miles), separated from the Turkish mainland by a strait only a mile wide. Its ancient neighbours were Ephesus to the north and Miletus to the south.

Samos the city, although very ancient (perhaps dating to the 10th century BC), went through the familiar cycle of independence, Persian rule, Athenian alliance, liberation by Alexander and eventual freedom in local affairs under Rome. It became part of the province of Asia in 129 BC. It has two celebrated antiquities: the Heraion – or sanctuary of Hera, the city's patron goddess – and the tunnel of Eupalinos.

The Heraion was rebuilt and enlarged several times, but its appearance now is a little disappointing, foundations, odd stones and one reconstructed column being all there is. Seek a knowledgeable guide, and avoid the over-attentive guardians who seem to believe that one's fundament will seriously damage any rubble one sits upon.

The tunnel of Eupalinos is altogether different. It was cut through a hill to facilitate an aqueduct. It is about as high as a man. At one side a deep slit has been cut, in which ran the water supply. The whole is about 1 km (⅗ mile) long, is straight, and was cut from both ends. The place where the two ends meet is almost perfect; your suggestion about how this feat was achieved will be as good as that of the most sophisticated archaeologist. The tunnel dates from about 500 BC; the name of Pythagoras is muttered in reference to its construction, but no one knows.

Stageira

Stageira was a small city made for ever famous as the birthplace of Aristotle (384–322 BC; see Part II, Ch. 6). It was attacked by Philip II of Macedon in 348 BC, but rebuilt by him out of respect for Aristotle, whom he had appointed as tutor to his son Alexander – the man who was to destined to end all Persian dominion over the Hellenes.

Stageira is halfway up the eastern side of the three-fingered hand that protrudes into the north Aegean from the Greek mainland, close to the junction of Macedonia and Thrace. The city occupies an isolated promontory surrounded by sea on three sides. Walls of the 5th century BC enclosed it entirely. On the landward neck of the promontory, the walls are still over 3.5 metres (12 feet) high in places, and 2 metres (7 feet) thick. Evidently, much of the city survived Philip's attack, but it never prospered afterwards, and by the time of Augustus, at the turn of the millennium, it was deserted. The place is wild, remote and well presented.

Troy

I have said what little I can on the immense subject of Troy in the first two main chapters of this book. At the site – difficult as it is to see properly – there are still traces of the *Iliad* story for those who have the eyes to see. Go with a good guide. The site is incomprehensible to an uninstructed view. Try to ignore the wooden horse where you enter: that story isn't even in the *Iliad*. And when you look over the plain of Troy – perhaps from the platform of the Temple of Athene – try to see the plain as an inland bay closed to the west (as it still is) against the Aegean by the Sigeum Ridge, but open to the north into the Hellespont. The Greek fleet would have sailed in from the north and beached against the Sigeum Ridge to the west.

The guidebook by Mustafa Askin is very helpful – as is he, if he can be found.

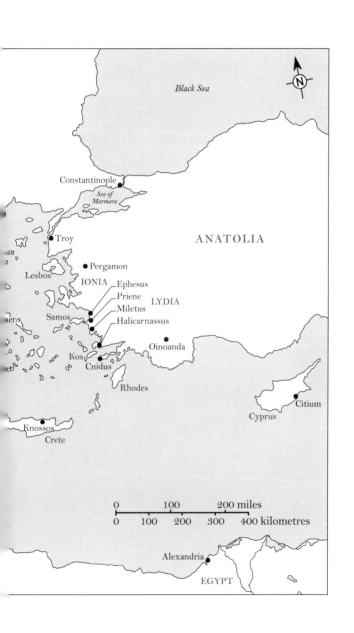

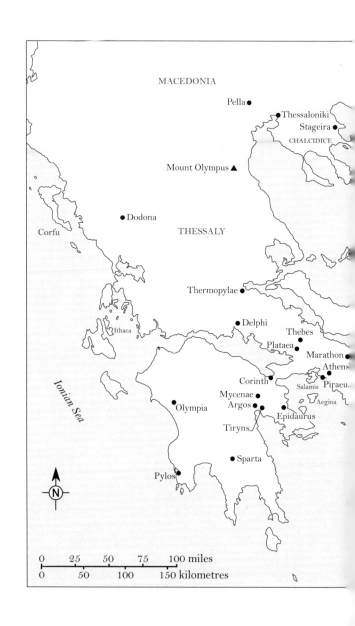

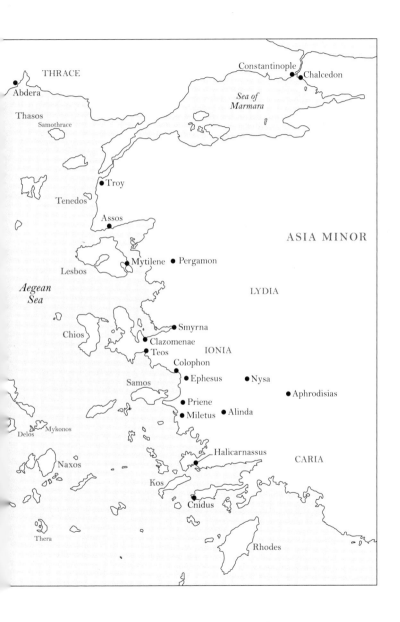

THRACE

Abdera

Constantinople ● ●Chalcedon

Sea of
Marmara

Thasos
Samothrace

●Troy

Tenedos

Assos●

ASIA MINOR

Mytilene● ●Pergamon

Lesbos

LYDIA

Aegean
Sea

Chios

●Smyrna

●Clazomenae
●Teos   IONIA

Colophon

●Ephesus   ●Nysa

Samos

●Priene   ●Aphrodisias

●Miletus ●Alinda

Mykonos
Delos

Halicarnassus

Naxos

Kos   CARIA

●Cnidus

Thera

Rhodes